A CROSSROAD DESTINY

 A catalogue record for this book is available from the National Library of Australia

© Vanessa Adelaide

Published 2023

ISBN: 978-0-6457505-9-1 (ebook)
ISBN: 978-0-6459332-0-8 (paperback)
ISBN: 978-0-6459332-1-5 (hardback)

Cover Image:

Greece, harbor of island Poros and Old Town by Arno Winter (CC3.0)

Published with the aid of Jumble Publishing and Editing (https://jumblepublishing.com)

A CROSSROAD DESTINY

by

Vanessa Adelaide

To the God who sees hears and understands all things.

Contents

Preface 1
Dedication 2
Chapter 1—The adventure 3
Chapter 2—The meeting 13
Chapter 3 – The decision 27
Chapter 4 – Conception 33
Chapter 5 – Goodbye 37
Chapter 6 – The suffering 42
Chapter 7 – God will provide 46
Chapter 8 – Getting closer 50
Chapter 9 – Support 53
Chapter 10 – The crossroad 59
Chapter 11 – Valentine's Day 73
Chapter 12 – New friends 75
Chapter 13 – Bruce 78
Chapter 14 – The proposal 85
Chapter 15 – The Brown family 89
Epilogue 92
Afterword 93
About the Author 94

Preface

I do not know what I may appear to the world; but to myself I seem to have been only like a child playing on the seashore, and diverting myself in now and then finding a smoother pebble or a prettier shell than ordinary, whilst the great ocean of truth lay all undiscovered before me.

Isaac Newton (1643-1727)

Dedication

Count your blessings may sound like a cliché but my hope is that all who may come to read this book may be stirred and encouraged to look inward and truly examine if they are truly living or barely breathing. Many of our real-life experiences can be the making of our destiny if we listen carefully. Although crippling and crushing as some experiences may be, the choice lies there for all of us. We all have the opportunity at these crossroads to look back and dwell, ignore or call out for help. Our darkest day can be used as a platform for greatness. Our mourning can be turned into dancing and our sorrows into joy.

Freedom may be achieved through forgiveness, loving our enemies, filling our minds with hope if only we choose.

Thank you to all who have crossed my path in this life, you know who you are and without you there would be no story to tell. Special thanks to Julie for seeing the need and being bold enough to meet it when you were called to and for my husband of 30 years. You will never be forgotten, and I will forever share my story, our story as it entwines with the lives of others and God himself.

My husband, your love and commitment to our family is like no other. You truly are a gift from God, and I will be forever thankful that you asked me to be your wife.

I can only hope and pray our children will one day imitate your great character and attitude towards life. I hope our daughter has the opportunity of spending her life with someone of your calibre.

Chapter 1—The adventure

It was ordinary June weather for London, crisp and somewhat cool compared to a southern hemisphere summer, thought Naomi. The strange triangular garden backing on to the train track at Winchmore Hill made her appreciate the open spaces of home. As she packed her bag for Greece, thoughts of home flooded her mind along with questions: Would she be safe there? What would her dad think? And what about Kay from next door, a single mum, would she envy her adventure or dread the very idea? Naomi would be leaving in the morning and now was not the time to change her mind. She had accepted the job and the very generous offer of a free ride to the Greek island of Poros, travelling through France, Luxembourg, Germany, Switzerland, and Italy. Being a romantic at heart, the sheer journey in the car would be enough to keep her excited about life for the summer.

On a cold, dark June Friday morning around six, Naomi got into the black BMW, fastened her seatbelt and began to wonder what the hell she had got herself into. Tony, her new boss, jostled and joked about trying to make the obviously nervous Naomi comfortable. Before long, Tony and Naomi drove off to take on the new business on the Greek island of Poros.

Driving to Dover was interesting enough. The idea of the car catching a ferry too as well as passengers inspired curious Naomi which led to her first foolish question, "So, do most English people drive to Greece in the summer?"

Green and totally naïve was an understatement, Naomi had confirmed Tony's thoughts about her.

Acting humble but rubbing his greedy hands together, Tony knew he had already profited by employing such a stupid tourist. The word vulnerable was not enough to describe her disposition right now. Tony looked at Naomi and his wicked thoughts danced with delight.

Poor Naomi had not an ounce of street smarts with no common sense at all. She had some confidence and her heart overflowed with adventure and dangerous optimism. Although 21, Naomi was a young 21. She had never lived alone and had hardly ever taken responsibility for herself. In fact, she had never shopped for her own groceries or washed her own clothing yet here she was being driven to Greece for the summer on a promise to contribute to the opening of the newest bar/café on the isle of Poros.

It wasn't until Naomi was in Switzerland that it dawned on her: Where was she going to sleep when they got there? What was the arrangement for her accommodation and wages? It had never been mentioned. When did she get a day off? Naomi was reconsidering her hasty decision to accept the job without any contract. What about the language barrier? She couldn't speak Greek. She did have one friend called Mary back in Western Australia who came from a Greek family, and she had once had a kebab after Club Atlantis in Scarborough at a Greek kebab shop. Remembering her experience learning Italian at high school, she reflected for a minute and realised that Greek was a completely different language.

Naomi was feeling very unprepared for the adventure but was also certain there was now no time to prepare herself for the biggest culture shock of her life. Naomi pondered out of the window of the car.

Tony was driving the car. She glanced at him and thought to herself, "Who is he?" She only knew him as the brother of a friend's mother's boss at the restaurant in Winchmore Hill. Naomi had been introduced to him one evening while dining there. Was he married? Had he been married? Did he fancy her—is that why she got offered the job? Questions flooded her mind and she couldn't sleep for fear of the unknown. She had assumed at the time he was just a businessman, but what sort of businessman was he?

They travelled together mostly in silence. Each time Tony pulled over on the side of the road for a nap, Naomi closed her eyes too and pretended to be asleep. As soon as Tony woke and started driving again, Naomi fell asleep. This happened all the way across Europe. Fear began to encompass her every waking moment; every cell of her body was weary and on high alert.

The scenery was spectacular, like scenes from *The Sound of Music*; everything was so green, and the mountains took her breath away. The beauty of the scenery relieved her fears momentarily.

In Bari, the Italian port, Naomi sat down, somewhat restlessly swinging her legs, on the bench waiting for the last ferry to take them over to Igoumenitsa in Greece. The ferry was running behind schedule and Naomi took out her note pad and pen from her backpack then walked over to introduce herself to some people she saw in the distance who looked her age. Naomi began to ask questions about Greece in the hope of connecting with some other tourists, but to no avail they did not speak English.

"Never mind," she thought to herself as she reflected on their friendliness and willingness to try. They just couldn't speak a word of

English and she realised she couldn't speak a work of Greek either. It was a stalemate.

She only wanted to understand the essentials, like *hello, goodbye, please* and *no, thanks,* and she thought this would help to pass the time. Without much effort, her friendly and approachable manner struck a chord with her fellow passengers and it wasn't long before they roared with laughter at each other and their cultural differences.

Her friendly and approachable manner though had two sides and it wasn't long before Naomi sensed an awkwardness with Tony. Initially, she didn't really understand what it was but it wasn't too long on the ferry before her intuition kicked in and her heart sank as she realised. Tony was a bossy, domineering, controlling and very manipulating man. He began to question her about talking to other passengers and Naomi felt his character had certainly changed the moment they took off from Bari, Italy. Entering Greek waters, she sensed a shift in Tony. It was clear there was a dark side to Tony, and she was trapped.

Trying hard not to show her fears at dinner, she chose the opposite to what Tony had recommended she order. It wasn't her usual evening meal but she coped with a stuffed tomato and sliced potato. "Weird food," she thought but so was this experience. To be honest, she was starting to think maybe she was weird too.

After dinner, Naomi politely excused herself and went to her cabin. Tony followed and aggressively asked her what she was doing.

"I'm going to shower and go to bed," she replied and, with that, she shoved the door closed and locked it in a panic.

Naomi made it off the ferry from Bari safely at Igoumenitsa. The drive through the Greek countryside from Athens to the port to Poros reminded her of the baren Western Australian outback. Australia seemed like another world away.

Their boarding onto the last ferry to the island of Poros came with a desperate urgency to get there. Tony stopped on the way to take in the beauty of the cliff tops overlooking the Mediterranean Sea. Despite being determined to present herself as brave, confident, and aware, Naomi thought, "Is this the end or the beginning of my adventure?"

As they drove slowly off the ramp of the jetty and onto the island of Poros, groups of children gathered and started screaming and began to chase the car with joy and cheers. Tony preened himself with this attention. The locals cheered and waved as they drove down the street. Somewhat embarrassed, Naomi hid her face and ignored Tony's nudges to wave back at the crowd.

Was Tony a celebrity? Well, if he was Naomi had never heard of him. It was evident though that Tony was well known and this brought a sense of peace to Naomi.

The smell of oily Mediterranean waters, the fumes from the ferries and the sounds of boat motors made her realise she was in a different environment now, very different from gloomy cold London. This was the place where her life was going to change forever.

The sounds of English tourists comforted Naomi and she began to relax as she realised contact with other tourists would be a daily occurrence while she was encountering Greek culture. This brought another sense of peace and comfort to her.

Only a couple of hours after arriving, Naomi met Sally and Kate, the two English girls with whom she would be working at the café. They had come over earlier and started to set up the business.

Tony showed the three girls the apartment which Naomi assumed was for the three of them. To her disbelief, Tony pointed out his bed in the room next to hers. It was now obvious to Naomi that Kate and Sally were very different girls to herself, very different, as they proceeded to get into their bikinis and cut-off denim shorts in front of Tony. Naomi saw Tony's delight and, with that, she took her purse and said she was going for a walk and headed straight for the nearest phone box. Before Naomi could even work out how to make an international phone call, Tony and the English girls were pulling up in the BMW in front of the phone box and shouting, "Get in, Aussie Lil."

Every slight measure of confidence, boldness and courage began to drain from her adventurous spirit. She was desperate to phone London and check out his character as it was becoming obvious to Naomi that she had gotten herself into a dangerous position.

That night, Tony paraded the three girls down the street and into a local Greek bar. To Naomi, it was like Sodom and Gomorrah. Never in her life had she seen such frivolity. She wasn't sure if it was a strip club or a public brothel. Fear gripped her as she sipped a Corona and one of Sally's English friends, sensing her discomfort, led her outside of the bar for some fresh air.

Lighting up a ciggie, Peter quizzed her about her travels and time soon got away from her as they talked outside away from the chaos and debauchery. She felt seen and understood for a short while.

It was not long after Naomi was back in the shared apartment and curled up in bed that her heart began racing. "Well, I am safe for now," she thought, trying to fall as eep and stop worrying about what tomorrow would bring.

Within a few days, Naomi had picked up a few local Geek words and learnt the names of some of the locals. Preparing and painting the café/bar was fun. Anything artistic and abstract always got her attention. With the sounds of *Simply Red* playing in the background while she learnt the art of making cocktails, Naomi tried with all she had to fight her sense of loss and isolation. Was she lost herself, emotionally, spiritually or was she just feeling isolated from her family and everything she knew?

Naomi thought about how she had asked her cousin to join her and how her cousin was quite happy to sit at home and do the same thing day in and day out. Comparing her situation but now enjoying the adventure, she continued to fight feelings of insecurity. Perhaps her cousin, Julia, was wise in her contentment.

In spite of her inner turmoil, Naomi continued wiping glasses and sorting out where to put what. Finally, the day came and the Zickni Café—café by day and bar by night—opened.

Naomi loved people and came alive after spending time with them. No matter who they were; if they were friendly, funny, or just simply had a heartbeat, Naomi could interact and feel happy, instantly forgetting her inner fears if she was with company. Other people's stories were always interesting to her. No matter what country, colour, creed, or faith they were from, if they were friendly or slightly warm, Naomi would claim them as a friend before too long. The downside of her personality, however, was that her naivety and gullible outlook lead her to err on the side of love rather than hate and to trust rather than be suspicious. She often thought she was loved when she was just used but that was a negative thought and that had to be denied because she believed in always trying to think positively which proved to be not wise on all occasions.

This weakness in her character eventually took her to a place she never dreamed she would go. While wiping down tables and making small talk to the customers, she had noticed out of the corner of her eye that Sally and Kate were constantly giggling. She watched them and took note but kept busy.

Sally and Kate had friends from London who had sailed to the island for the summer season. They were reasonably young men, handsome but somewhat snobbish. They were short in conversation, somewhat aloof, and cold.

After being introduced, Naomi reflected on what sort of people they were. They were so full of themselves. She wondered what sort of young people would sail from London to Greece for the summer—what would that cost? She worked out their age and decided that they obviously came from wealthy families. She thought that there was really nothing substantial to talk about with them and they were not her cup of tea. What sort of young Englishmen had their own sailing boat?

Starting work at three in the afternoon and finishing at three in the morning, she was always exhausted but she still accepted every invitation from customers to go clubbing after work. She needed the freedom and the choice to interact with people she wanted to, people she felt comfortable with.

It wasn't long before she made it a habit to go clubbing every night after work. "How unique," she thought, up on top of a mountain overlooking the Mediterranean Sea, filled with tourists and the sounds of fantastic dance music. Naomi loved it.

It was an awesome nightclub and she was a great dancer. She enjoyed being on top of the stage and, even more, she enjoyed the recognition of being a good dancer. The nightclub opened at the front and overlooked the sea. After the occasional dance, she would light a ciggie and chat on the patio. She was young, free, and loved dancing and meeting new people. The atmosphere was electric and the crowd so much fun. There was a mix of tourists and local Greek people. She had pizza after closing and then returned home, sometimes after the sun had risen.

Naomi slept until about 11 in the morning each day and then, before she knew it, it was time to get ready and return to work day in and day out. After a few weeks without a day off or a break, Naomi thought it was finally time to ask what was going on. What were her actual working conditions? She decided to ask Tony and, with some struggle, a very disgruntled Naomi finally got a day off—the day off she had been longing for and which came with such difficulty.

Naomi couldn't believe Tony's audacity in offering her a day off only if she went out to the olive groves in the mountain with his friend, Nico. Nico was a slimy, greasy, sleazebag at least 25 years older than she was and couldn't speak English. What was the intention? What was this all about?

"What a nerve," she thought as she left the café.

She was glad she had told him where to get off and that there wasn't a chance of her going anywhere with Nico. Still, Tony was making her feel like a hired prostitute and she was getting more and more frustrated with his control and hold over her life.

"Why did Tony want to know my business?" she pondered. "He asks question after question: Where was I going? Who was I going with?"

As she reflected, it became clear that Tony was asking for too much information. It was absolutely none of his business—all she wanted was a day off. Was he planning something? Who the hell did he think he was? His controlling personality was beginning to weigh her down.

With her Walkman and beach towel, sunnies on her head and sunscreen in hand, she walked down to Askeli beach and sat with some Dutch tourists she had met previously in the café. After not even sitting down for five minutes, she heard Tony's BMW driving slowly along the beach to see if she was where she said she would be.

"This is too bloody much," she said to herself as she dived into the sea. "I have got to get out of this."

Chapter 2—The meeting

One afternoon on her way to work, she stopped into another café called The Rendezvous.

"Hello," she said as she walked towards the bar addressing what looked like a group of English tourists.

"Hello," said a voice in a very familiar accent.

"Well, you must be from Liverpool," she said to a tall blonde man around her age.

"Yes," he replied, "and where are you from?"

Naomi proceeded to tell him how she was from Australia, but her parents were originally from England and not too far away from Liverpool.

He seemed intrigued at her accent, and they seemed to click from that quick introduction. There were other tourists in the café that afternoon; however, it was Tom who caught her attention. After a quick chat and a glass of coke, Naomi continued walking up the hill to work. Tom followed with another girl, and they chatted amongst themselves as the girl walked ahead of them.

Back at Tony's café, Naomi was asked that when clearing all the tables to empty any ice cubes left in the glass into a bucket. Sally told her they were going to rinse and reuse the ice cubes.

"How disgusting," said Naomi.

Kate added they had a hard time freezing the water in Greece. Somewhat boggled but too shy to question these girls, Naomi retreated inwardly and was off in her own fantasy world when she heard a familiar voice.

"G'day, Naomi."

It was Tom from The Rendezvous café putting on an Australian accent. Pleased to see him, she smiled and said, "Hi, there."

Naomi poured Tom a beer and he watched as she chatted and served other customers. Naomi chatted to Tom in between serving and told him what Sally and Kate had said.

"They're taking the piss out of you, Naomi," Tom informed her. She had sensed they might have been but in her own naivety she had convinced herself that nobody would be that cruel. She was wrong.

Later that night at the nightclub, Naomi ran into Tom again. They danced, chattered and smoked ciggies together on the patio. Naomi felt she had found someone to talk to about Tony and his controlling personality and her perceived dilemma. She shared some of her fears and frustrations with Tom but mostly she really enjoyed his company. He was funny.

One reason Naomi did not want to leave Tony's café was her mail. She received letters and cards from home and it was her only source of comfort. Naomi knew if she left Tony's it was very unlikely she would receive her mail. Her mail was very important to her right now.

"Listen, I'll come in each week and collect it for you if you want to leave," Tom said, trying to offer some help. He felt sorry for Naomi. He thought she was stupid, and he was baffled at her naivety. Tom was still trying to work her out for himself.

"I might do that. I will let you know and thanks," Naomi said as she walked away.

After giving it some thought, she made the decision to pack her belongings and leave the apartment around half past two in the afternoon. Tom had suggested that no one would be in the apartment at that time and Naomi believed it was safer to leave a note for Tony than try to reason with him about how she was feeling. "Besides, he wouldn't listen anyway," she thought. His hot-headed ego would not care if she complained about the job or the conditions. Naomi knew he would only manipulate and dominate her in conversation and she felt she could not stand his personality and ego for one more day. She was done. He was way too much to handle.

By leaving this way, it would mean she would not arrive at work at the expected time of three and it would give her enough time to walk with her suitcase down the white staircase and into the village centre. She hesitated as she realised she only had enough money for one night's accommodation.

Carrying her suitcase down the hill to the village centre, the handle snapped on her suitcase and the tears began to roll down her sunburnt cheeks as she struggled to carry it. As she persisted down the hill dragging her suitcase, she saw in the distance a man walking towards her from the entrance of the village. It was Tom.

"You've done it then?" he said, trying to comfort her and lifting her suitcase onto his shoulder. "Here, I'll carry your suitcase. Where are you going?"

"The first hotel will do and then I'm off to look for another job," she shared through her tears.

"Looks like you need another suitcase too," laughed Tom.

They walked into the lobby of the hotel and Naomi booked a room for the night.

"Thanks for that," she said, walking Tom outside.

"Where are you going to get work?" Tom asked, a little concerned.

"I don't know—anywhere. I'll get something," she said with her natural optimistic attitude, trying to believe her own words as she spoke them to Tom. Tom believed her. He thought this girl could do anything; she was bold and friendly and appeared quite independent.

Soon after checking in, with no time to waste, Naomi walked through the streets of Poros, stopping and chatting to the locals and the friends she had made during her time there. She heard a girl call out her name from another bar. It was a Dutch girl who had a Greek partner. The partner and his family owned a bar on the island. In the summer, Demetrio and his brothers would go across to Poros from Athens and run the bar for the season. The rest of the family would take ferries over and spend the weekends there. Tina had met Demetrio on her own personal adventure to Poros four years earlier and she had lived in Greece for some time. Her English was quite good. Tina was a friendly girl and Naomi had warmed to her the first time she met her.

"Why aren't you at work, Naomi?" Tina asked.

Naomi opened her heart and shared her dilemma with Tina.

"Just wait here for a minute," Tina said and went up to the family apartment via the outside stairs on the right side of the building. The apartment overlooked the patio garden in front of the entrance to the bar and had wide open windows through which Tina's mother-in-law often watched the traffic of tourists walking by when she wasn't cooking for the family.

Before long, Tina's mother-in-law was calling out from the apartment above the bar and waving at Naomi to come up. Within minutes, Tina came down to where Naomi was sitting in the patio area and they went up the stairs together and into the apartment.

Tina's mother-in-law said something in Greek and before long they were sitting down and eating some of Tina's mother-in-law's lasagna. Naomi was hungry and without money until her next job and she was more than grateful. She was going to have to ask for money in advance at her next job as it was, so the lasagna was very appreciated.

Within an hour, Demetrio was there and Naomi was offered a job with the lovely Greek family. Her job was to open the bar in the afternoon, DJ and manage the bar until later in the evening when the Greek brothers would arrive and take over the music. The family provided Naomi with accommodation and she was shown to a small room left of the upstairs apartment where she could sleep and keep her belongings. Naomi was relieved and grateful to be starting work later that afternoon. It soon became apparent there was no bathroom, only a trough and bucket in a funny looking outside laundry.

It was summer and Naomi decided she could cope with cold water washes. Standing back and sizing up whether she could fit her whole body in the trough, it became obvious she couldn't and she realised the neighbours could see straight in. Naomi worked out a way to keep her dignity and wash daily. After being scolded in Greek by a neighbour, she soon understood that washes could only occur before two in the afternoon as the water proceeded to flow down the white staircase and onto the floors of the neighbouring cafés and bars underneath. It was okay before two because the heat of the day dried up the water before the businesses began to set out the table and chairs after siesta. Business usually started around half past three.

In the hot, balmy summer nights with outdoor bars overlooking the sea, the sounds of traditional Greek music and people laughing loudly, Naomi was entertained wherever she went. There was no such thing as a boring night in Poros.

Naomi began to feel more at ease with the weight of Tony's overpowering personality lifted from her and the freedom at Demetrio's bar. She was really starting to enjoy the summer on the island of Poros.

It wasn't too long before she bumped into Tony. Abruptly, he asked, "What are you doing? Where are you working?"

With quick, short answers, she politely told him she was not his concern, and she was quite happy with her new arrangement.

"I would appreciate it if you would leave me alone," were Naomi's last words to slimy Tony.

By now, Naomi had worked out how to make an international phone call and contact had been made with her family in Australia.

"Don't spend too much," she heard while dialling home in the phone box. It was Tom in the barber's getting his haircut. The phone booth was right outside, and he could see her through the mirrors.

"I haven't got much to spend," Naomi replied and they both laughed.

Tom and Naomi's paths were crossing constantly, and Naomi was beginning to feel emotionally attached to Tom. They were birds of a feather and wired the same in many ways. He was warm and easy to get along with.

Drinking iced coffee together before work, they arranged to meet the next day early and go to the beach together for a swim. That night after work, Naomi resisted the temptation to go out. She went straight home to sleep so she could get up earlier than normal to meet Tom.

The next morning, they met at the designated beach. They spent the morning swimming and walking along the beach, climbing over rocks and telling each other jokes. On their last swim, a small boat was anchored just left of the rocks and this appealed to Tom.

"Hey, I'll race you to the boat," shouted Tom.

Naomi tried her best to swim fast and catch up with him, trying her best to demonstrate her athletic ability.

"How can he be so good at swimming coming from Liverpool?" she thought as he raced ahead.

"Shall we climb in and have a look?" he suggested.

"Oh, no, I couldn't," said Naomi. "What if someone saw us from the shore?"

It was deadly silent on the boat and Tom climbed aboard.

"What a great view from here; this must be a Greek fishing boat," Tom said, and, with a cheeky grin, he put out his hand to help Naomi up onto the boat.

No sooner had Naomi sat down in the boat then a voice from the top shouted, "Hey, what are you doing?"

Tom dived in and left Naomi for dead. Naomi dived in and followed him, embarrassed, cursing Tom all the way back with each stroke to the shore. They were both as adventurous as each other. It was obvious they both enjoyed each other's company.

"I've been married before," confessed Tom.

"Oh, how nice," Naomi replied awkwardly. "You must have been very young."

"Yes, I was 19 and I was in the navy," he said.

Naomi shared she had never been married and had only been in love once as a young teenage girl.

They spent the day getting to know each other and it appeared that both of their guards were down after opening their hearts. The foundation for a deep friendship was established.

"I'll see you at work. I'll pop in later and we can go out after you finish if you like," invited Tom.

Going their separate ways, Naomi smiled to herself. She was growing to like Tom a lot and trying very hard not to fall in love with him. She laughed as she remembered her neighbour Kay's warning, "Don't be like that girl in the movie *Shirley Valentine*."

Wiping down the tables early that evening, out of the corner of her eye she saw Tom enter the courtyard. With a smile, she acknowledged his presence and took a tray of shooter glasses inside the bar.

Tom wandered over to her and whispered, "Would you like to sleep at my apartment tonight? I share an apartment with three other people. I'll ask Diana if it's okay. She's an Aussie like you. I think you will like her."

"Okay," answered Naomi.

Later that night, Tom introduced Naomi to Diana. Bursting forth with laughter at Diana's quick wit and dry sense of humour, Naomi thought, "At last, this is someone who truly understands where I'm coming from."

Although Diana was from Melbourne and Naomi from Perth, there was a definite connection.

Diana was a lot like Naomi in some ways. She was adventurous, funny, and strong-willed. Compared to Naomi though, Diana was more self-confident and much more independent. Her father had given her a credit card to travel with in case she got stuck, just in case. Naomi wondered if this support from her father also gave her confidence but she didn't let that thought last for long as Naomi had a new job and new place to live and she thought she was financially okay. Diana had a social wisdom which attracted Naomi and resulted in her warming to her quickly. They swapped stories and adventures, including laughing at cultural differences while enjoying their youthful freedom together. Diana shared with Naomi about a time she spent in the south of France before coming to Poros picking grapes for a famous winery and living with an eccentric artist in a mansion.

It really wasn't too long before a mutual trust was built between the two girls; a trust that would take them beyond this season of their lives.

Swimming laps of the hotel pool, soaking up the sun and planning their night out after work, the girls soon gathered a group of followers. Like two pied pipers together, they drew a crowd.

"Safety in numbers," thought Naomi as she applied her lipstick for work. Things just couldn't be better.

"I really love you," said Tom, out of the blue.

Staring straight at him, Naomi tried to count how many beers he had had.

"Will you have a son with me?" he asked.

"How ludicrous," thought Naomi, startled.

"Thank you for the offer and no," was her reply.

Fear gripped her for a moment followed by an elated sense of joy for the offer. Naomi thought to herself, "I'm travelling, I'm young, and I'm having way too much fun for such a responsibility."

All night Naomi reflected on what Tom had said. It was the first time a man had spoken these words to her. She felt flattered but unsure. Who would ask that?

Thinking about her next-door neighbour back in Australia who was a mother at the age of 20, it scared the pants off Naomi, and she tried to put it to the back of her mind. "A mother at 21," she thought. "No way."

She dreaded the thought of ever being a mother, let alone a young mother at that. Still, she kept thinking about the words Tom had spoken. They were powerful and had hit her heart like an arrow.

Naomi never mentioned it again but the thought of what he had said interrupted her thoughts constantly. Missing home and having feelings of insecurity about her future, she decided to call home. To her surprise, her dad had just won some money on the Aussie Lotto. It was a Sunday and her dad was in quite a strange state. He had realised he was a winner the night before but had to wait until Monday morning to find out exactly how much he had won. He wasn't on his own as he was in a syndicate with 11 other men at work. He had only started his job two weeks prior, and he had taken the place of a long-term employee. He was rejoicing but was feeling somewhat awkward for Bill who had worked for the firm for years and had played Lotto each Saturday with the syndicate. He was considering sharing some with Bill and already contemplating what he might do with his winnings when Naomi called from Greece. After chatting with Naomi, he decided to go to Greece to see his daughter once he knew how much he had won.

Straight off the phone and back down to the café, Naomi was beside herself, not knowing if she was the daughter of a now millionaire or if the amount won would affect her at all. Naomi did not care either way. This was just good news for her dad.

That night after work, without any thought, Naomi shared the news with Tom. She bought a bottle of expensive champagne and shared it with her friends at the bar in celebration. Showing off but also knowing she had to wait until Monday, she tried to forget about it by dancing and spending time with Tom, Diana, and new friends.

Diana and the entourage joined in celebrating the elating news and together they celebrated their youth with long late nights dancing, drinking and laughing.

There was still plenty of summer left in the northern hemisphere when Isaac, Naomi's dad, arrived. The weather reminded him of Australia straight away as he stepped off the ferry. Meeting her dad again was exhilarating for Naomi. It had been a while and she had so much to tell him. It was good to see him again and they could enjoy the summer and celebrate on Poros.

Naomi introduced Tom to her dad, and they got on famously straight away. Tom helped Isaac to find accommodation. They spent time together while Naomi worked. It wasn't long before Isaac had overindulged and he was quite seriously drunk when Tom came to the bar and informed Naomi, "Your dad is in a bad way. I've just dropped him at his apartment, and he nearly fell of the motorbike. I had to hold him up and try and ride the motorbike one-handed."

Tom referred to times in the navy where he had seen men drink too much and he was worried. "I have laid him on his side, and I think we should go and check on him when you finish work," he said.

Embarrassed and worried, Naomi left work early and together they went to check on Isaac.

"Does he do this often?" asked Tom.

Wanting to say no but telling the truth, Naomi said, "Yes; sometimes."

"He really should look after himself here, you know. Anyone could take advantage of him and steal his passport and his money," Tom said.

"I know," answered Naomi. "Maybe he is celebrating his win."

Naomi was too scared to ask her dad how much he had won, and she was not sure now that she wanted to know. She was beginning to think it must be more than he could handle. He had not brought his girlfriend, Annie, on the trip which Naomi knew was a recipe for disaster. He could get out of control and, with money to burn, she knew it could end in disaster. On the flip-side, it could also mean he didn't win much at all and couldn't afford to bring Annie. Naomi was too scared to ask now and tried not to talk about it. There was one thing though—Tom knew but she wasn't sure this was a good thing. Tom wouldn't do anything stupid, surely?

Tom was beginning to write Naomi poetry and love letters like no man ever had. Was it only a holiday romance or was it something else? The connection between them was intriguing; however, Naomi was not completely convinced of his love for her. He was spending a lot of time with her dad and Naomi was beginning to have second thoughts.

Naomi confided in her dad, and he offered her advice she would later reflect on, "Just don't get too emotionally attached to him."

"It's too late for that," she thought as she sat down next to her dad on the ferry to Hydra. She was really looking forward to spending time with her dad and this day out was just what she needed to clear her head and think about her life.

Was Tom the one for her? Could she ever say goodbye to him? He felt like family, but she had only known him for three months during one of the most adventurous times of her young life.

Walking around Hydra with her dad and using his new camera, Naomi smiled for photos next to donkeys, fishing boats, stray cats, and cafés. She was trying to enjoy the day with her dad, but she was constantly distracted by the words Tom had spoken to her. Was she in too deep? Had he already stolen her heart?

The tourists came and went week after week. Soon it was time to see her dad off at the jetty as his holiday had come to an end. Waving goodbye and blowing him kisses, Naomi hesitated, wiped the tears from her eyes and pondered for a split second whether she should be going home too.

As the Mediterranean summer season was coming to an end and the tourists were beginning to leave the island in their droves, Naomi knew it was the end of a different kind of season in her life. She felt sad but didn't really know why. The village grew smaller in numbers and the conversations changed to picking olives and working on the vineyards. Naomi was torn between staying on or going back to England. She finally decided she just could not say goodbye to Tom. Her heart had become attached to him more than she wanted to confess. Having family in the same part of England made it very easy for her to return to England. Tom had mentioned he was going home too. Naomi had enough money for her airfare and a not a cent more. Tom and Naomi said goodbye and Naomi left him feeling unsure about his feelings for her now. The tables had turned!

As Tom headed back to England the following day, the last words he said to her were, "I'll see you there."

Tom mentioned he had no money at all and was planning to hitch a ride from Athens to France, hopefully on a truck. Naomi thought nothing of this and said goodbye.

Chapter 3 – The decision

As the ferry sailed out late in the afternoon, the weather was still warm. The cafés, restaurants and shops along the water were all looking so empty now. The fishing boats dwindled in the bay and there were more people leaving than arriving, even the beach cats looked lonely.

Sitting down at the window seat, Naomi reflected as she thought about the last six months of her life—what an adventure! As the island grew smaller the further the ferry sailed, Naomi felt smaller on the inside too. Naomi considered and paused, looking at the island behind her: Was it her destiny to have met Tom or was it just a fleeting season in her life?

Two other girls on the ferry sitting opposite her noticed her daydreaming out to sea and interrupted her thoughts.

"He really liked you, you know," said one of the girls.

"And right from the start," added the other.

Both girls had been at The Rendezvous café the very first day they had met. Listening but not responding, Naomi continued to stare out at the disappearing island of Poros.

As the island completely disappeared, the thought of Tom did not disappear from her mind. He was certainly stuck in her thoughts, ingrained in fact.

By now she was feeling like *Shirley Valentine* and a bit foolish too. Naomi could not deny the connection she had made with Tom. Here was the beginning of another season, one where she could put him out of her mind forever if she chose. Thoughts of him and their time together were just not disappearing.

Pondering her future without Tom, she could not get away from the fact a vibration of the heart had taken place and he had certainly left a mark. They had communicated on many levels physically and emotionally. Their souls had connected. Would this soul connection remain if their friendship was to end?

Philosophising about human beings and their profound and amazing ways of touching deeply, she asked herself the big question, "What have I got myself into?"

Up until this point, Naomi had never allowed herself to fall in love, not after the first time as a teenager. Naomi always managed to stay aloof until now. Was her frozen heart starting to melt?

Arriving back in Athens, at the airport she lined up with a group of English tourists and waited for a last-minute cheaper flight. Within hours, she was on a flight and on her way back to a cold winter in England. She was going back to a cold season of weather and, little did she know, it would also become a very cold season of her life, one that no amount of human connection or spark could ignite.

Finally back in England at her aunt's house, she collapsed on her cousin's bed and began to tell her of her adventures in Greece.

"Julia, why don't you venture out while you are young?" she asked.

Secretly, Naomi was quite envious of her cousin's simple contentment in life. Compared to Julia, Naomi was restless and desperate to find her place in life.

Julia and Naomi were the same age and were very close considering Naomi had spent her life in Australia. Julia was sensible and cautious.

After being back in England for a few days and already bored and bothered by the cold weather, Naomi rang another relative. While chatting on the phone to Debbie, Debbie's friend asked if Naomi would like a job as a telemarketer at a fitted kitchen shop in Liverpool. Without giving it any thought, Naomi accepted the job. She could not sit still for long and was always willing to give anything a go. As she accepted the job, she remembered that Tom lived over the water in Liverpool, and she wondered if he had made it back from Greece yet. "Maybe he lives near the shop; maybe I'll bump into him," she thought as she sat on the train journeying to her new job.

Tom lived over there all right and within hours of starting her new job the temptation to call him was overwhelming, especially sitting there with a telephone in her hand all day. It was the perfect recipe for what was to come.

Tom sounded surprised to hear her voice but was intrigued. By the end of the day, he had come down to the shop and they were reacquainted.

"I don't live far from here," he confessed. "Would you like to come over and meet my family?"

Naomi was excited and misjudged him on that invitation. He was interested in her, it seemed, and besides her family was originally from the same area. Her parents had immigrated to Australia which was something Tom had contemplated doing since he was a young lad in the navy. His mother's family had immigrated to Canada and Tom had dreams of moving away from Liverpool one day. Something deep inside him knew there were great opportunities for him in life and he knew they were not in Liverpool. He didn't know where, but he did know they weren't where he came from. Tom loved Liverpool and its rich history, but his heart was continually stirred to move on and discover new places. The travel bug had haunted him since his days in the navy.

Tom was drawn to Naomi. There was something about her he liked but there were other things that made him want to run a mile. Naomi's over the top personality was embarrassing; well, in his hometown anyway. His mother had pointed out that they were alike and together they could be either a lot of fun or very dangerous.

"The two of you," she said after the first introduction, and she roared with laughter.

Could there be two stars in a relationship? In a family? In a household? He really wasn't sure this would work in Liverpool, maybe in Greece, Australia, or Canada but not here.

"This girl was too much," he thought and he began to reflect on his old girlfriend, Lesley. He wasn't sure he was over Lesley and he began to miss her now he was back at home. Comparing the two girls, he was beginning to wonder whether he had made the right decision. Tom had gone to Greece with his girlfriend for the summer and they had broken up while there, just before he had met Naomi. Thinking about it, he began to realise he was in a very awkward situation.

"Let's go to the museum on Sunday," suggested Tom.

"Okay, that sounds interesting," said Naomi.

Week after week, he showed Naomi around Liverpool and entertained her with his wit and humour. Naomi's grandmother had been born in Liverpool, and she felt closer to her family roots while Tom showed her the city. She appreciated the history and insight Tom had about the city. Standing outside the grand church one Sunday morning, they stopped and read the headstones on the graves outside the church building. They contemplated the war and the great men and family members who had gone before them. Naomi thought about her uncle who had left the port of Liverpool and died in World War Two, never to return home, and another uncle who had set off to New York from Liverpool and made a life in the USA.

Naomi felt connected to the city and was daydreaming about her roots when Tom interrupted her thoughts.

"Oh, look at this grave," he pointed out. "A baby. How awful!"

"Yes, it is. I had an Aunty who died of diphtheria at the age of eight I wonder where she's buried. My poor grandmother—three children gone," Naomi said.

She was thinking about her dad and his only other surviving brother when a voice interrupted them both and an old man invited them to come into the church.

"No, thanks," said Naomi and she turned to Tom. "Let's go to the pub."

"Are you sure you don't want to go in and have a look?" asked Tom. "I think it will be very interesting. I think they are having a special service."

"No, thanks," Naomi said again. "Let's go to the pub."

The following Sunday, they ventured out in the afternoon and found themselves at the great chapel of Liverpool which was another amazing building filled with rich history. The sound of the choir echoing outside drew them in that morning. Entering the grand building, they sat together at the back row and listened.

"Lovely singing; so pure," said Naomi.

"Let's go," said Tom and together they got up and left the church, both stirred and uncomfortable.

Naomi's birthday was coming up and, with the money he had won in Lotto, her dad paid for her mother and sister to surprise her on her 22nd birthday. They flew in from Perth and straight to her grandmother's home in Birkenhead. It was an unannounced visit and a complete surprise for Naomi. She immediately rang Tom after what she had thought was only going to be an invitation to her grandma's for a cup of tea.

"Wow," said Tom. "That's amazing. I'll head over and met them tonight."

Laughing at bingo with all her family, Tom was reminded again of Naomi's fun-loving, outgoing personality. He enjoyed her company and thought she really was good fun. Her family were nice too and, yes, definitely from this part of the world with the same sense of humour and wit. Drinking his pint and laughing, he was convinced he was lucky to have met Naomi and now he felt warmly connected to her family.

Chapter 4 – Conception

After a long day out in Liverpool and coming home from work, Naomi really was not up to visiting her Uncle Eric and Aunty Gwen with her family. Everyone was going though—her mum, her sisters, her cousins, her aunty. This was her mother's favourite uncle and aunty, and everyone knew they were always so hospitable and so much fun. Naomi hesitated and at the last minute changed her mind and said she was going to run a bath and go to bed. She was just about to put her toes in the bath when the phone rang, it was Tom.

"Hi, what are you doing tonight with your family?" he asked.

"Nothing, I'm exhausted. Just staying in," she said.

"Shall I come over?" he asked.

"Sure," she said.

"I'll see you soon," Tom replied.

Naomi hung up the phone and got back into the bath.

When she was sitting downstairs and watching TV, there was a knock on the door. It was Tom.

They sat and chatted about the events of the day, and it wasn't long before they were laughing and experimenting with different accents. They had both enjoyed theatre arts at school. Their sense of humour and talent for accents had them both amused for hours.

"So, are you going back to Australia with your mum and sister?" he asked.

Looking at Tom, Naomi said, "No, I'm having too much fun here."

Later, not being on the contraceptive pill as she hadn't been sexually active, Naomi knew she had taken a risk. The atmosphere went quiet for a moment before Tom said, "I think we have just made a son," and lit up a ciggie.

"Don't be crazy," said Naomi.

Weeks went past and Naomi became tired of travelling to Liverpool for the telemarketing job. Restlessness was part of her nature. She tried to find herself another job closer to home. Her determined attitude landed her two new jobs, one in a nursing home for the elderly within walking distance from where she was staying and the other one in an upmarket boutique. She loved both. They were so different from each other that they were enough to keep her interested, busy and earning money. Besides the more money, she made the longer she could stay in England.

Tom picked her up from work one night and began to tease her in the car about her chores in the nursing home.

Laughing, she said, "You know what? I've been feeling a bit sick lately."

With a knowing look and glare, fear filled Tom's eyes as he investigated her gullible face.

Drinking a pint together at the pub in their matching jeans, Tom turned to Naomi and said, "Finish this and we will go to the chemist and get a pregnancy test."

"I won't be pregnant," she said.

"No, come on. Let's get this sorted," said Tom.

Naomi climbed the stairs to the bathroom and Tom followed. After testing herself and waiting, she heard Tom urgently ask, "Well, what does it say?"

"Oh, my God! It's positive," yelled Naomi.

Picking her up and swinging her around, Tom gave nervous Naomi a big hug and kiss on the cheek. Naomi went strangely quiet while Tom was elated.

"Well, who shall we tell first?" asked Tom. "Do you want to ring Australia or come and tell my mum first?"

Not really wanting to do either, Naomi said, "Let's go to my grandma's."

Driving to Naomi's grandma's, Tom joked around and presented as very pleased with the idea while Naomi was in complete shock.

"Is this the first grandchild for your mum and dad?" Tom began and then interrupted himself. "Oh, this baby is going to be so spoilt."

"Grandma, we have something to tell you," Naomi said as she took off her coat and gloves. "We have just found out I am pregnant."

"Oh, dear. Perhaps you had better ring Australia," her Gran offered.

Tom's facial expression gave Naomi the courage to ring home.

"Go on," he nudged and she made the call.

"Dad, it's me. I'm pregnant," she said.

"Well, you had better get married and come back to Australia quick," her dad replied.

While having a cup of tea at her grandma's, it was obvious to Naomi that her grandma was embarrassed; however, her grandma responded to them in her usual graceful, positive, loving and very polite manner. They waved goodbye and headed straight off to Tom's parents.

Walking through the door and straight over to his mum on the couch, Tom said, "Mum, we have got something to tell you. Naomi's pregnant."

"I know", replied his mum. "I knew this was going to happen the first day I met her."

"How weird," thought Naomi and she thought about what Tom had said on the night of conception and then the instant reminder of his question at the bar that night in Greece when he whispered in her ear, "Will you have a son with me?" She was now completely freaked out.

Chapter 5 – Goodbye

Considering her dad's idea about coming back to Australia, they planned a day trip to Manchester to Australia House. Tom was interested in understanding what was needed to immigrate. Naomi was born in Australia, but Tom wasn't sure he could relocate permanently.

Naomi was moody and quite rude to the lady at the front desk that day. Tom was embarrassed at her lack of manners and respect for the staff at Australia House. They had taken a trip there to inquire about immigration and visas for Tom to Australia. Naomi was nervous and Tom demonstrated no real understanding of what she was going through.

After arriving home, Naomi was clearly troubled. "What the hell have I got myself into?" she thought.

She really wasn't sure she was ready to be a mother but when is anyone ever ready? And how does anyone know they were ready to be a parent? Didn't they have to be married first? Thinking about the population of the world and if anyone was ever ready to multiply, she continued to question the idea. Do people just have babies or do they plan for them? If everyone planned for a baby, maybe the world would not be so populated. It wasn't as f it was a terrible situation; just a new one and she was feeling very much alone in the experience.

Naomi pondered, "Well, I have six months of my life left."

Selfish thoughts entered her mind. She had always honoured young mums but never understood how they had got themselves into situations but now she knew how it could happen. Her heart was breaking for her friend, Kay, in Australia who had gotten herself pregnant on a one-night stand and who she had judged but, comparing her situation, she comforted herself, sighing, "Well, at least I'm not a single mum."

Absolutely nothing was accomplished in Manchester that freezing cold day, just lots of paperwork, information and confusion.

"Who can be arsed with all of that?" thought Tom secretly as he drove Naomi home.

It was while she was cleaning Beryl's room in the nursing home that Naomi decided she had better resign from her role, the heavy lifting and bending might not be good at this stage of her pregnancy. She really did not know but got a feeling she should resign.

"Seriously," she thought. "What do I know?"

She had never been pregnant before and she really was just guessing.

Thoughts flashed through her mind to Australia. It would be summer there now and she imagined Mullaloo Beach packed with people. She paused as she thought she could smell the sunscreen and taste the salt water for a long second.

Looking back at Beryl who was 101, she sat on the end of Beryl's bed and decided perhaps Beryl would have 101 years of knowledge to share. As Naomi proceeded to share with Beryl the news of her pregnancy, Beryl's face lit up with joy.

"Oh, love," she said as she grabbed Naomi's hand. "I am so happy for you."

She stared into Naomi's face and she said, "And guess what? So am I!"

Naomi snapped back to reality and remembered she was working with dementia patients who could not possibly give her any advice. She was better off talking to one of the mannequins in the dress shop than any of the patients in her role at the nursing home. Naomi was feeling isolated and alone.

Standing at the bus stop after a shift at the nursing home when it was minus two degrees, the wind was so cold her ears began to burn. Her legs too, even wrapped in tights with thick jeans over the top. She was aching with cold.

The Christmas lights were up at the mall and the decorations were beginning to brighten the gloomy city. Carols played in every shop and the shops were beginning to fill up with Christmas shoppers. Naomi loved the experience of the pre-Christmas English atmosphere.

Standing at the entrance to the boutique, hearing the song *Going Home for Christmas* by Kenny Rogers, she broke down. Sucking back the tears at work, she began to feel so alone and so confused. While smiling at customers and staring at the mannequins, she soberly acknowledged that it had been days since she had heard from Tom.

Sitting on the bus on the way home was always a time to reflect on the day. She decided it was time to tell Debbie and Bob her news. Naomi was staying with them and had been putting this conversation off because she knew the right thing to do would be to move out and, at this stage, she didn't know what was happening with her and Tom relocating to Australia.

She had called Tom a couple of times and his mother had said each time that he was at football practice and that she would pass on the message regarding her call.

Four days after she had left a message, Tom called.

"Naomi, I don't think I love you as much as I said I did and I think you should go home to Australia and get on with the rest of your life," he said.

Sliding down the wall and falling on the floor in a heap, Naomi replied, "You don't really mean that, do you?"

"I do and I'm sorry. Goodbye," he said.

She checked how many weeks pregnant she was and realised that, according to Qantas, she had three weeks in which it was safe to fly before she would not be allowed and would then have to stay in England and have her baby, alone and scared.

"He has got cold feet," thought Naomi, as she packed her suitcase with optimism. "He will follow me. I just need to give him space."

Saying goodbye to the girls and staff at the boutique was sad. She really had enjoyed working there and she reflected on the jokes in the staff room and the warmth of English company as she resigned. While finalising her details to fly home to Australia, she received a phone call from two friends, Mel and Dean, who had arrived in England for their trip and adventure. They were in the area and had just bought a camper van.

"Come over," invited Naomi. "I have got some news to share."

Naomi opened the front door and welcomed them in with a warm hug and Aussie high-five. Naomi began to pour out her heart when Mel interrupted with "Oh, just get rid of it and keep travelling with us."

"No way," Naomi replied. "This is a life we are talking about, not a social inconvenience!"

Waving goodbye to Mel and Dean, Naomi was furious.

"Evil bastards," she muttered under her breath. "How could I ever live with myself? This is my child. I will go home. Tom will follow, I know it."

With what seemed like no support from anyone, she held back her deepest fears until the taxi had turned the corner and she cried all the way to the airport. Waving to Debbie and Bob and looking through the side mirror, she felt a deep sadness.

Naomi smoked and drank scotch on the plane in denial. This was all a horrible nightmare; it's not real; it's not happening, she tried to convince herself. Sitting next to some other young Aussie tourists returning home from their own adventures, it began to sink in that she really was pregnant and very much alone. Naomi started to feel ashamed and very angry.

In between a bout of crying, Naomi tried to pull herself together by going to the bathroom to wash her face and reapply some makeup. Once again, she looked in the mirror and reassured herself it was okay. It was just a temporary situation Tom would follow; of course, he would. He just had cold feet. It was probably her attitude the day they went to Manchester. "I was rude that day," she confessed.

Naomi tried to gain her composure before the plane landed knowing her friends and family would be there to meet her on arrival. The plane landed on time and, with her shoulders back and head held high, she began to walk thought the arrival gates at Perth International Airport. There they were, every one of them, the people who cared: Her parents, her sister, and even her next-door neighbour, Kay. Megan was there too and everyone else who meant something to her.

Chapter 6 – The suffering

The Australian summer was still in full swing, and the beautiful days kept her mind off her situation. Naomi spent most of the time at Mullaloo Beach, walking up and down and thinking through her decision to return to Australia on her own over and over.

By now, her pregnancy was obvious and her little bump was starting to move and kick. Laying hands on her stomach, she said to her unborn baby, "I don't have much but I do love you. I will always love you together we will be okay."

Naomi was becoming a familiar face at the beach daily and decided to enjoy her last single motherless summer topless and tanned.

Knowing she had no material provisions for her baby, Naomi took on a couple of days of work. She worked with her neighbour, Steve, driving him around. Steve had lost his driver's licence and needed a driver to run his business. Steve had his own business and had to go from place to place every day. Naomi needed the money and Steve needed a driver so it worked well for both.

It was after her ultrasound that Naomi fell in a heap again. It wasn't being pregnant that distressed her, it was being abandoned, rejected and the seriousness of this. It wasn't only about her, but her child. Their child was entering this world soon and the arrival was uncertain. Was Tom going to be there? Could he surprise her like the time her mother and sister did when they came to England for her birthday? Naomi knew all things were possible, although this time it wasn't looking good.

Naomi had been back in Australia now for two months and she hadn't heard from Tom and she wasn't sure she would. Still remembering his phone number off by heart, she called it.

Toms's mother was pleasant enough on the phone, but Naomi reflected afterwards it was probably a very awkward phone call for Pam to receive. She did remember Pam saying to keep in touch and that she did want to know how she got on.

It was here Naomi broke down and went next door to Kay and Steve's place.

"That frigging mongrel," said Steve. "Where does he work? Where does he live? I'll find the mongrel and give him an ear full."

Steve was wild not just in his chosen language either, but in every sense of the word.

Knowing it wasn't the right thing to do really but feeling emotionally at the end of herself, Naomi gave in and allowed Steve to fuss over her and make international phone calls tracing his whereabouts. Tom was a bus driver now and no longer living at his parents'. But Tom McDonalds were a dime a dozen and Steve's quest for verbal revenge failed.

Her doctor advised that Naomi attend Lamaze classes with other women due to give birth around the same time. Naomi thought this would be a good idea and, besides, Dr Carol had flirted with her and said if he was a pregnant woman he would want to look like Naomi. A graduate doctor from Victoria, he had apparently flirted with other young single mothers and shared his stories about returning on the weekends to rural Victoria to assist his family to birth calves. Although not sure whether to be flattered or insulted, Naomi loved the attention.

Naomi took his advice as she felt she was so ignorant and wondered how the hell the baby was going to get out. She was desperate to be educated in this area and knew her experience was not going to be the same as that of a cow.

The Lamaze class was at half past six and Naomi arrived 10 minutes early. Parking her car in the car park, she noticed she had 10 minutes to spare and thought she would wait in the car. It was raining outside, and the car was warm.

Naomi sat and watched couple after couple, hand in hand, walk through the double doors of the centre. Some men were carrying pillows, others had their hands on their wives' shoulders while others were rubbing the backs of their partners as they opened the door for their pregnant women.

Like a thunderclap, she screamed and broke down. Starting up the car and yelling, "Why me?", she squealed her wheels in the wet rain, did a burn-out and took off down the street in tears.

"I am young, I am attractive, I am funny, I am kind, I am friendly, I am nice," she yelled, "and I am clever."

A voice from her inner conscience echoed, "Well, you are not that clever—getting yourself pregnant and dumped!"

Naomi had always looked down at teenage pregnancies and single mothers. She used to think, "What's wrong with them? Don't they know how to love?" Now she found herself in the same situation. Was it that love was just not enough?

"What does my future hold?" she thought as she cried on her bed. She put both hands on her stomach and said, "I am sorry, my baby. I love you. No matter what happens, I will love you with all my heart."

She stroked her pregnant stomach until she fell asleep.

Chapter 7 – God will provide

"A hundred dollars was a lot of money to get your fortune told," she thought but, desperate, she paid it. Naomi needed to know her future. She was going crazy and losing all hope. She was no longer the happy, optimistic, and friendly girl she once was. Thoughts of suicide entered her mind and more than once; she needed answers and quick.

Collecting second-hand junk and bits and pieces from family and her friends' throw out piles, she set up a stall at the weekly swap-meet.

"I am selling old junk for money," she told herself.

"How did I get here?" she asked as she emptied her car.

Time was drawing near for the arrival of her baby, and she didn't have a single item of clothing, or a cot, a pram or any of the other things needed for her baby. Her stall was a weekly event. Heavily pregnant, she pushed on. She had no other option. Waking up at eight months pregnant at half past four in the morning, filling her car with junk and setting up her stall ready for the early morning onslaught, Naomi had no idea she shouldn't be lifting heavy boxes and doing the things she was doing. She had refused to go to Lamaze classes, and she was too scared to read any books on pregnancy. With no support, there was nothing else she could do.

Her mother's nasty words had penetrated her heart, and she pondered on what she had said to her the night before, "Naomi, what are you going to do for a pram or a cot?"

Naomi had replied with, "God will provide."

"Where did that come from?" she questioned herself. She wasn't religious and her parents certainly weren't either. Her mum had told everyone in a drunken stupor at the pub about Naomi's situation and now Naomi felt betrayed by her own family too. She felt ashamed and embarrassed now everyone knew that she had gone to Europe for an adventure and returned pregnant with no father, no husband, and no sign of one.

Soon, old friends and boyfriends had got wind of her situation and visitors began to arrive. Cameron took her out for dinner and grieved for her.

"You shouldn't have gone to bloody England," he said, trying to comfort her at Sizzlers. "They're all bastards."

He didn't understand everything that had happened, and Naomi didn't have the strength to share the whole story. Besides, he was just expressing his disappointment for his old friend. He honoured her for going through with the pregnancy on her own, with no money, no possessions and what looked like no hope. Cameron was adopted and had always appreciated the decision his natural mother had chosen. He popped in now and then and kept his eye on her. Cameron was a patient at the chiropractic clinic Naomi worked at. They were the same age and good friends, although never intimate but always available for each other after a relationship break up. They felt like family to one another.

Eric from school came over. He had always fancied Naomi, but he was not her type, although they were still friends all the same. Eric and Naomi had lived in the same town as teenagers and shared experiences living in outback Western Australia..

After a visit from Eric, Naomi came back inside and noticed an envelope on the dining table. She cleared away the coffee cups and opened the envelope. There was $500 and a note. The note said, "Buy something for your baby, like a car seat or a pram, and keep your chin up, Naomi. Love, Eric."

Earl had visited too in the same week. He was the brother of her friend, Bronwyn, who she had initially travelled to Europe with. They had gone their separate ways just before Naomi had taken the job in Poros. Bronwyn had shared her situation with Earl, and he had come around just to be nosey, although they had no real connection.

David had dropped in, stoned and with not much to say, but she knew this was his way of showing support. David was another old friend who was also adopted and she guessed this was too much for him to process straight. He had done what he could with all that he understood when it came to complex situations. He took the time to visit her; that was the best he could do.

It was at an invitation to Paul and Nicole's wedding where she finally got to wear the cocktail maternity dress she had bought while working in the boutique in England.

Naomi loved Nicole. They had met when they were 15. Nicole's dad had taken a job in Perth and relocated from Sydney. Nicole had left her friends in Sydney for Perth and Naomi had left her friends in Kalgoorlie for Perth. Naomi and Nicole had met at business college the year they turned 16. Nicole had returned to Sydney at aged 19 and Naomi had visited her every summer since. They had a special friendship so she checked with Dr Carol and he confirmed Naomi could fly to Sydney for the wedding. So, with the money Eric had left her for her baby, she purchased a ticket to Sydney for Nicole and Paul's wedding.

That restless adventurous spirit was still trying to rule her life.

"You selfish girl," her mother yelled. "Are you really going to use that money on a trip to Sydney?"

"I don't care about material things," Naomi screamed back. "And it's my baby, not yours. We will be fine; I will be back in time to have my baby."

Another bout of denial was presenting itself.

"Screw it," she thought as she sat on the plane, trying to justify her decision. "I am not giving up my lifestyle; besides, I am only going to a wedding."

This decision did mean that she only had two more swap-meets until the baby arrived. Would she have everything she needed, she questioned herself. She muttered under her breath, "God will provide."

She had said that before. She wasn't just trying to justify herself. Something deep down inside her actually believed what she was saying. "Where did that thought come from?" she wondered.

She said it over and over, "God will provide."

Chapter 8 – Getting closer

It was very encouraging for Naomi to see all her friends in Sydney. During her time visiting Nicole in Sydney, she had also become very good friends with Nicole's friends, and it was great to see them all again. Since going to Europe, Suzi had gotten married to Bob. Suzi had met Bob on a trip to Hawaii and had married him there on the beach. Bob was a surfer from South Carolina and had relocated to Australia to be with his wife. A holiday romance with a different ending to Naomi's. Looking at the photos of Bob and Suzi's Hawaiian wedding, she could see the wedding looked very romantic, very simple, very Hawaiian and very Suzi. They had just had their first baby, a girl named Kailani, a Hawaiian name to signify their love for each other and their hope for their daughter.

Naomi couldn't help but think about her situation. It couldn't be anything other than completely opposite to Suzi's. Happy for Suzi, though, she kept positive and continued looking through Suzi's photo album.

Naomi was excited to see Sharon. Sharon had married Tony, her first love and boyfriend since 19. They were also expecting their first baby, just a month before Naomi.

Eliza was married, Nicky and Carolyn were still single, but they weren't pregnant either.

Naomi stayed with Carolyn at her Nan's place and together they all went to Eliza's parents and watched as Nicole and her bridesmaids got into the bridal car.

"Are you okay?" Carolyn asked, holding Naomi's hand.

"Yes, I'm fine. Doesn't she look beautiful?" Naomi commented as her eyes followed Nicole into the wedding car.

Carolyn was a sensitive soul and very thoughtful of others, especially her friends. Naomi had warmed to her on her first trip to Sydney. Her tender motherly heart and empathy was exactly what Naomi needed right now.

Thinking of Naomi, Carolyn led them to seats at the back of the church. Sitting down together as the wedding song began, Carolyn chose to look straight forward as she touched Naomi's hand. Carolyn tried to compose herself as she considered Naomi's grief and just kept looking forward. Carolyn was grieving for Naomi right now and couldn't bring herself to look at her.

Tears trickled down Naomi's face at the torment of seeing love stare her in the face.

"Perhaps I should have brought a pram for my baby," thought Naomi, wiping her tears and blowing her nose in the church.

Nicole was pregnant too and due around the same time as Naomi. Paul had asked Nicole to marry him, and this only reminded Naomi of her situation.

By the end of the ceremony Naomi's face was bright red, her mascara smudged and her sobbing uncontrollable.

Comforting words from Carolyn and Suzi brought Naomi around and before long they were at the reception sitting alongside Sharon and Tony, Simone, and other Sydney friends. The table seating was fantastic and perfectly arranged. Naomi was with all her favourite friends, and everyone was enjoying themselves.

Naomi managed to dance and cheer along with the fun of the occasion, forgetting about her own situation for the time being.

On her fight back to Perth, she pondered when the next time would be when she would see her friends in Sydney. She dreaded to think of it. She knew her life was about to change forever. Thoughts of moving to Sydney flashed through her mind. She did have a core group of caring friends there. She had a few weeks left until her baby arrived and, besides, she still did not have any furniture Should she? She could probably get a flat there and a single mother's pension. She loved the northern beaches of Sydney. She had always felt a strong connection to the city of Sydney and the girls there. These thoughts led her to phone Suzi.

Chapter 9 – Support

After chatting on the phone to Naomi, Suzi sensed Naomi's need for love and support. Within a couple of days, Suzi, Bob and baby Kailani took off from Sydney in their old car and headed straight for Perth. The five-day drive was nothing more than a miracle. Driving across the Nullarbor in their old car, they could hardly believe they made it themselves and were shocked it even got over the Sydney Harbour Bridge.

"On a wing and a prayer, we made it," said Suzi.

Suzi was a lot like Naomi. She was filled with optimism and loved adventure. Wild at heart just like Naomi , she was always willing to have a go, to try something new and put herself forward with a smile.

After meeting Naomi, Bob confirmed to Suzi that Naomi was special, and he understood why they were good friends. Bob and Suzi agreed to relocate. They had just arrived back to Sydney from Hawaii, and he hadn't been able to get any work and staying at Suzi's parents was getting squishy. Bob and Suzi agreed it was a great time to head to Perth before they got settled themselves. The timing was perfect.

Bob and Suzi kept it a surprise and did not call Naomi until they were in Western Australia.

"Hey, girlfriend. What ya doing?" Suzi asked.

"Folding washing and getting fat," laughed Naomi.

"Well, don't make any plans for tomorrow. We will see you at your place about four."

"What?" yelled Naomi "Where are you?"

"We are in WA and on our way to your place, honey, and we are here to go through the birth with you if you like," Suzi said.

With an emotional outburst of gratitude, the tears flowed down Naomi's cheeks as she expressed her excitement to Suzi, "I love you, Suzi."

"Love you too, Naomi. See you tomorrow," Suzi replied.

Naomi's mum did not even question the idea of accommodating three more people in her house. Jan knew Naomi was falling apart and needed all the help she could get.

Naomi was stuck in traffic that afternoon with Steve and was late for Bob and Suzi's arrival. Driving into the driveway, she laughed. There was Suzi who had made herself at home. She had blown up a swimming pool and filled it with water in the front garden, parked their car on the side of the road, set up a tent and bought a carton of beer. There they were, sitting on their camper chairs, waving, as Naomi pulled up with Steve in the driveway.

Embracing Suzi was a Godsend. Naomi felt loved and supported finally in her hour of need. Bob took care of Kailani and Suzi and Naomi walked along the beach and had a heart-to-heart.

Rubbing her back, Suzi said, "You are going to be fine. Everything will work out. You will have a beautiful bubba next week and you will make a great Mama."

"Thanks, and I am never having sex again until I am married," Naomi said and finished off the conversation.

Suzi didn't judge but, somehow, she knew Naomi meant it. Suzi thought to herself, "Mmm, we are a different generation," but wisely kept her thoughts to herself.

Phone calls from everywhere kept coming day after day now. Her best friend, Sharnie, from Kalgoorlie rang and said she would come to the birth.

It was at her 40-week check up with Dr Carol that the alarm bells rang.

"You have extremely high blood pressure and protein in your urine. Your kidneys will start to fail if we are not careful," he said.

The news added to Naomi's fear.

That afternoon Naomi was admitted to hospital for pre-eclampsia.

"Good," she thought. "At least I will be safe when labour starts."

She was ten days late and it was advised that they break her waters and induce the labour.

A nurse has come to inform Naomi at eight in the evening that at 10 that night they would be breaking her waters and by 11 she should be in labour and by the morning her baby would be born.

"Shit," thought Naomi as she escaped the ward. Wandering off to the other end of the hospital, wanting to escape but knowing there was no way out of this now, Naomi found a private bathroom with a large bath in it.

"I wonder what this is for," she thought as she turned on the tap and began to fill it up. She locked the door and got undressed and got into the bath. She began to try and forget what the nurse had just told her was going to happen. Naomi closed her eyes in the bath and tried to deny the nurse ever spoke to her.

There was a knock at the door and Naomi just stayed still and hoped they would go away. Then the sound of keys unlocking the bathroom door alarmed her and she sat up to the night cleaner who was coming to do the rounds. Apologies and embarrassment lead Naomi to get out, dry herself off and return to her ward. Arriving back late, the nurses were perplexed. They were not too sure how to handle Naomi.

Refusing to answer their questions, Naomi glanced over at Sharnie who was sitting on a chair next to the bed. Sharnie asked the nurses if Naomi and her could have a few minutes together in private.

"Oh, come on, Naomi. It's not that bad. The baby has to come out. I brought my camera, and I can take photos if you like," Sharnie said.

It was 10 that night when they broke her waters and began to induce Naomi. Naomi screamed like a mad woman and they wheeled her out of the ward and into the birthing suite. It wasn't because she was close to giving birth but for the peace and quiet for the other mothers who had recently given birth. Fear gripped Naomi as the labour pains began. The nurses were concerned for her mental health.

Jenni's mum, Helena, came in. Jenni was one of Naomi's best friends and Helena had been close to Naomi throughout the pregnancy even after Jenni and her new husband, David, had moved to Chicago. Jan, Naomi's mum, and her sister, Rachel, were standing outside the birthing suite as well. It was beginning to look like a support team for a sporting match.

"This is very impersonal," thought Naomi as she sucked on the gas in between contractions. They all got the hint and only Sharnie and Helena stayed to support her.

Thinking about angels and New Age invisible healers, Naomi went very quiet, focused, and in the present moment. At three in the morning, five hours later, her baby boy was born at 6 pounds and 9 ounces and 33cm long.

Naomi shed tears of joy as she was overwhelmed with feelings of love and elation combined with hope. This was the beginning of a brand-new day. A whole new world. A healthy good-looking, long, delicate, precious, little baby boy. Naomi's sorrow had turned to joy. Her first-born son was here, and all was well.

After being wheeled in to have a shower, she was then wheeled back into a double-bedded room. As she got out of the wheelchair, a tall lady with a radiant smile and beautiful glow approached her.

"Hello," she said softly. "I'm Julie. I heard you screaming in labour, and I have been praying for you."

Naomi embraced Julie and held on to her loving arms as if she knew her intimately.

"I remember you from Lamaze classes," said Julie. "My husband and I have been praying for you ever since. I am a Christian, I have just had a daughter and we have called her Emma. We are sharing this room together. Are you feeling alright?"

Although just having had a baby herself, Julie embraced Naomi like an older sister. It was a very special embrace. It felt like a welcome home hug.

"What are you going to call your son?" Julie asked gently.

"I don't know yet, maybe Alexander," Naomi said.

Bravely, Julie asked, "Are you on your own?"

With a straight talking, "No, I am not," Naomi bowed her head down and stroked her baby's head. "We are not alone," she lied.

Julie knew she was lying but left it at that.

Lovingly gazing at her son, Naomi asked, "What shall I call you, my precious boy?"

Several names came to her mind. She thought about giving him her dad's name, but something stopped her.

Her quiet time with her newborn son was constantly interrupted with visitors and phone calls. Naomi was beginning to feel like a circus clown and desired some space. She continued to smile bravely at every visitor and held her deepest, inner-most feelings to herself.

It was Geoff's visits to Julie and their daughter, Emma, that cut her up inside. Watching the way he took photographs and cooed to his daughter and the way he loved his wife was enough to make Naomi want to die. She lay searching her heart for answers.

"Why me?" she sobbed.

She slept and dreamt of being married, being valued and being honoured only to be woken up by a nurse checking her blood pressure.

The rejection was taking hold of her now and she began to feel the weight and sorrow of her situation. Her heart was heavy with grief. There was no bouquet, any number of flowers or kind words that could help comfort her now. These were the darkest hours of her life. Holding her baby close, she caught a glimpse of light through his perfect little face. A small snapshot of hope for the future.

Chapter 10 – The crossroad

"Billy," said Naomi's dad. "We will call the baby Billy. Whatever you call him, Naomi, I am calling him Billy."

Naomi struggled with this; this was her son and yet it seemed he was named by someone other than his parents for a moment.

"I like Willem," thought Naomi. "I am going to name him Willem and Billy can be his nickname."

Taking Willem home to her mother's was a special time. Learning to nurture this precious child began to do Naomi's soul good. For the first time in her life, her life was not about her alone. It was as if this baby was given to her to begin the softening of her selfish heart. Her heart was becoming tender, loving, and selfless.

Her next-door neighbour, Kay, had also just given birth to a little girl, Kylie. Together, they breastfed their babies on the couch, walked and talked. Naomi was grateful to be going through these early baby stages with someone. Steve was very good to her too, always checking in and helping where he could. It was his sense of humour that brought tears of joy to Naomi and so she was content living next door to Steve and Kay, even if it meant living with her mother.

A phone call to Tom's mother seemed liked a waste of time. Naomi thought she would call and let them know the baby had arrived and that it was a boy. Pam seemed quite friendly on the phone but in Naomi's heart she knew there was now a great divide between the two families. Trying not to dwell on this, she struggled to move on.

Infuriating anger rose in her being one night and she could not rest with this unresolved situation. Her friend, Sharnie, had taken very personal photos of her in the birthing suit which had annoyed Naomi. Naomi felt belittled now on every side.

During her fit of anger, she took an envelope popped the photos inside and addressed then to Tom's parents. Walking Willem, she dropped them in the post-box in anger and battled angry thoughts as she pushed the pram.

The next morning, she awoke to the gentle cries of Willem and wondered for a split second whether she had dreamed she had sent the photos or whether she had done what she thought she did.

Overwhelming shame flooded her whole being. Stunned at her own actions, she began to break down again, knowing she could not retrieve them from the post-box.

She was wallowing in self-pity on the couch when there was a knock on the door. It was an unexpected visit from Julie, her hospital room-mate.

"I have some things for you in the car," Julie offered. "We thought we were having a boy and collected lots of blue *Peter Rabbit* clothing. Would you like them?"

Wrapping her arms around Julie, Naomi began to weep. Naomi welcomed her inside and accepted the bags of clothing from Julie. After Naomi made coffee, they sat and chatted while their babies slept. Naomi opened her heart and shared her story.

"I can call in again if you like," said Julie.

"That would be nice," thanked Naomi and they said goodbye.

Things were getting a bit uncomfortable at her mum's and Naomi wanted her own space. Her mum was only trying to help but with all the traffic and constant visitors from the patrons at the pub, Naomi had had enough. Her mother worked there and often brought different people back after work and the constant partying and singing was taking its toll. Naomi had changed. She was finished with this lifestyle and now she longed for a quiet place to raise her child.

Naomi's dad had just been offered a job in the northwest and offered an opportunity for Naomi to move out of her mother's house.

"I'll do a deal with you," said her dad. "If you look after my three cats, you can live here rent free. I need to take this job up north."

Naomi loved living in her dad's house in Mullaloo. It was a lovely place to be. She could hear the waves crashing at the beach at night and she felt at home there. It was privacy and peace at last for the price of a few tins of cat food a week.

The lively, energetic, fun-loving Naomi was disappearing. She was becoming a recluse very quickly. She secretly hated the cats and kept them outside as much as she could. She didn't trust them around Willem and besides they gave her hay fever.

One day while she was putting out the cats, there was Julie pulling into the driveway on another welcomed surprise visit.

"Oh, no," she thought. "If only I knew she was coming I would have put them out the back door."

Naomi let Julie in and, before long, she was glad she did. There was something special about Julie. Naomi couldn't quite work out what it was she liked about Julie. She radiated love and care. Naomi warmed to her charismatic, fun-loving, genuine heart.

It was the offer of a picnic that made Naomi squirm.

"Oh, no, thanks," she said. "I haven't got enough petrol."

"Oh, no, we will pick you up," suggested Julie. "I will go now and get some fruit from my folks. They just live around the corner from here. Dad has a mobile fruit market. He goes from door to door selling his produce."

Naomi's face lit up. She knew Julie's dad. He was a lovely old Polish man, so gentle, so warm and so kind. Julie was just like her loving father.

Later that afternoon, Julie and Geoff came and picked Naomi and Willem up and took them along to a picnic.

Just as Naomi had imagined, there were couples with babies and small children and again Naomi felt like a slut; however, it was Geoff who offered to take Willem for a walk and another man pushed Emma alongside. Together, Naomi watched as these men took her baby for a walk and with that Naomi and Julie went for a walk together.

"You know, Naomi, God loves you very much," Julie began.

"Here goes," thought Naomi.

Julie continued, "He has a plan and a purpose for your life. Jesus died on the cross for our sins so we can be forgiven and have eternal life."

"We are all sinners," explained Julie. "There is not one person on the earth who hasn't sinned."

Naomi wanted to puke. She could not run off if she wanted to as Geoff had Willem and she and Julie had walked in the opposite direction to the men and babies for a chat.

Hardening her heart for protection, Naomi questioned and quizzed Julie with her arms folded on the outside and on the inside of her mind.

Julie went on to say, "I have been married before. Geoff is my second husband."

Somehow this part of Julie's story got Naomi's attention.

"I was unfaithful to my first husband," Julie went on, "and a terrible pot smoker."

As Julie opened her heart and shared her scars more deeply, Naomi began to engage intensely. Listening closely and feeling more comfortable, they continued to walk back to the picnic area.

'Why don't you come to church with us tomorrow?" Julie asked.

"No, thanks. I go to swap-meets on a Sunday and try to make a bit of money," answered Naomi quickly.

"Okay," said Julie and politely left it at that.

Julie and Naomi became very good friends. Julie spent many days with Naomi teaching her how to cook and even spent a night at Naomi's house with her baby one night when Naomi needed her support.

Throughout the summer months, they would take their babies to airconditioned shopping malls for hours, sometimes the whole day, just to stay cool and so their babies could sleep. Neither of them had airconditioned houses and in Western Australia the summers were horrendous.

Julie was funny. Even though she was a Christian, she had a great sense of humour which Naomi welcomed. Somehow, after a bit of time, Naomi's concept of what it was to be a Christian began to change. She had her own ideas and what that meant and her friendship with Julie began to change her perception around Christianity. Naomi admitted she was wrong.

"Christians are just people who have had an encounter with Jesus Christ. It's not a tradition," she thought. "People who somewhere along life's journey, whether through tragedy or circumstances, have been interrupted with a Holy interruption. That was it—a Holy interruption."

Julie was constantly introducing her to her church friends and Naomi liked every one of them. Some were ex-drug addicts, others ex-criminals, ex-prostitutes, ex-homosexuals and other society outlaws.

The time came when Naomi accepted an invitation to go to church. This time, she was moved by Geoff and Julie's offer to pick her up and, when they arrived, they had purchased another baby seat and had it fitted into their car. There was one for Emma and one for Willem. Sitting in between the two babies, Naomi nervously endured the car ride to the church. She felt dirty and awkward.

It was the shiny faces of the people in the church that moved Naomi. They were all happy-looking and friendly. People took their children to one side of the church to an organised nursery for kids. Nervously, Naomi left Willem in the hands of unknown women. They looked friendly and a bit too nice, Naomi thought.

Sitting down in the church next to Julie, the music began. The words of the songs they were singing came up above on a large screen to the left of the stage. People burst forth with singing, singing with all their hearts with their arms raised high and eyes closed. Looking around, Naomi felt confronted and guilty. She tried to blend in and sing too but her tears overwhelmed her, and her grief surfaced yet again. Not understanding anything but knowing one thing for sure, Naomi knew these people knew God and she didn't. The words of the songs frightened her yet the people surrounding her did not seem frightened and were singing them with peace and great, bold joy.

They finished singing and a man got up and talked about things that went over her head. A shiny bowl passed by and she watched as people put money into it. The sermon went over her head, but it was the end of the church service that pierced her soul.

"Jesus died for the lost and the broken-hearted," the man declared. "Is there anyone here who would like to receive forgiveness and receive Jesus Christ as their Lord and Saviour? Raise your hand if this is you and I will pray with you."

"Jesus died for the sinner and the ungodly," he went on.

With that, Naomi thought, "That's me," and raised her hand as she bowed her head. Going forward to the front of the church, Naomi felt slightly embarrassed but looking upward to heaven, she knew it was the right thing for her to do.

After the church service, Geoff and Julie were so excited for Naomi, they organised a barbecue at their place.

Weeks went by and Naomi still did not fully understand the enormity of her decision. Believing in God was easy for her, especially after giving birth. The miracle of giving birth was enough for Naomi to believe in a Creator. The whole process from conception to birth was incredible, something she would never understand fully.

Believing in God, love, was easy but believing in the devil was not so convincing for Naomi.

Naomi had spent a lot of time and money on fortune tellers and books on astrology in the hope of learning about her future. One lady tried to convince her these practices were evil and the power behind them was one of witchcraft. Naomi politely listened but had never been one to believe in ghosts or anything to do with science fiction. It wasn't her thing; it was too out there. Besides God was now all she needed, He was love and everyone was a friend. She continually tried to see the good in everyone despite her experience. Having mercy on the poor was easy for Naomi. She has always had time for the down and out and for those who were less fortunate.

Wrapping her baby in a blanket, Naomi was reminded of a time when she was coming home late from nightclubbing and had seen a homeless man curled up on the bus-stop bench. She remembered how she had taken a picnic blanket out of her car boot and wrapped up this old homeless man at three in the morning without any fear and driven home with a small sense of satisfaction.

Showing love and grace was easy for Naomi and these thoughts led her into her bedroom and she flopped on her bed, the tears again began to flow. "Why doesn't someone love me?" she thought.

"Oh, God," she cried out for the first time. "I am so sorry for having sex outside of marriage."

Praying through her tears, she believed she had brought her broken heart on herself. Convinced of her bad choices, she bowed her head to her knees.

A strange yet familiar voice entered her bedroom, "If you will put me and my kingdom first, I will add all of these things to you."

In what seemed like a second, she saw a tall, large figure of man dressed in a long white gown with a lantern in one hand and his other hand clenched in a fist so as to look like he was knocking on a door. He had a long white beard and appeared to know everything about Naomi, very gently but with a definite authority inviting and warning her all at the same time.

Before she could catch her breath, Naomi's tears came to an abrupt stop. With a very strange knowing, Naomi knew Jesus had entered her bedroom. Standing up and opening her curtain, she knew she could not deny what had just happened. She had two choices: She could walk outside and forget what had just happened or stay and ponder the truth that she had just had her own personal experience with the God who created the heavens, the earth and everything in it.

But what did that mean? She had never really read the bible and so she phoned Julie who confirmed that what Naomi had heard was indeed a holy scripture from the bible. Julie could not get to Naomi's house quick enough.

Julie and Geoff arrived and while Naomi put the kettle on. Geoff was walking around her house from room to room. Naomi did not know what he was doing but assumed it must be for her good and so she didn't question him.

During a coffee, Julie tried gently to convince Naomi of the evil behind astrology, numerology and fortune telling. Julie shared holy scriptures in the book of Deuteronomy 18, verse 14, where God talks about forbidding some of these practices. Still, in Naomi's mind she resisted and wondered if this was just Julie's opinions on these matters.

Waving goodbye, Naomi felt secure and at last filled with hope. Her thoughts were now focusing on the hope and love that God had offered her. Besides, she did not dabble in any of the areas such as astrology any longer.

Being fully immersed in God's love for her, she thought, "Does this mean if I pray for Tom, he might come to Australia?" as she looked down on Willem and changed his nappy.

That evening, she decided for the first time to go to bed with all the lights turned off in her house. Up until now, she had a fear of the dark and being alone in her dad's big house at night with just Billy, having a few lights on helped her feel safe. But Naomi was safe in God's hands now and she believed in Him more than her fears.

So each switch from the front door of the house to the back bedroom went off, one flick at a time. Naomi got herself into bed and the last light to turn off was her bedside lamp.

"One, two, three," she counted to herself and, with that, she confidently turned off the lamp.

"No more fear," she whispered to herself as she rolled on to her side. Within a matter of seconds, she sensed someone standing at the door of her bedroom. Who could it be? The doors were locked and God was on her side now.

With her heart beating fast, she boldly turned on the lamp. To her horror, there stood a small man, like creature no taller than the level of the door handle glaring at her. He had a cone-shaped head, slanting eyes and a look that she had never experienced.

"Jesus, help," she called out, asking for divine help and not blasphemously cursing his name. Instantly, the creature disappeared, and a strange sense of peace covered her.

"Wow," she thought. "I think I have seen an evil spirit."

Focussing on the power in the name of Jesus to rescue rather than reflect on the experience, she drifted off to sleep.

Sometime later in the night, Naomi woke again this time to her bed being rattled and lifting on the ground.

"Jesus," she called. "Holy Spirit, Father God, what do you want? Are you waking me up to pray?"

Picking up the Good News Bible that Mrs Murgatroyd had given her, she tried to find some comfort but didn't know where to look and so with that she lay back down on her bed.

Naomi was now convinced of the unseen realm. The angels were real and now she knew so were devils.

The next morning after Naomi had checked the letter box, the front door stuck open and in raced Queenie, her dad's favourite cat. She ran straight through the house, past the kitchen and right into Naomi's bedroom.

"How strange," she thought. "The cats never come inside and never in such a hurry."

Queenie ran under Naomi's bed and stayed there. On bended knee, Naomi leant down to grab the cat and noticed a book she had been reading months earlier lying on the floor, right in the middle of the bed. Lying flat on her tummy and commando-crawling, Naomi reached the book.

"At last," she thought with the cat in one hand and the book in the other.

Walking the cat to the front door, she let her go and looked closer at the book she held with two hands. It was a very popular and very thick astrology manual. A revelation from heaven washed over her and she began to tear it up in pieces. Reflections on her experiences from the night before further convinced her of the scripture in Deuteronomy

Julie had shared. Naomi was now convinced of both good and evil, Jesus and Satan, angels, and devils. Naomi tore the book up from front to back, page by page. She began to believe in the unseen powers of good and evil.

Naomi was in a great place now and she just about believed it. Pondering on God's love for her and this supernatural promise which aligned with these holy scriptures Julie had pointed out, Naomi decided to take a trip to the Christian bookshop to purchase her own bible.

Strapping little Billy and singing two lines of the only Christian song, she knew she drove to Koorong Christian Book Shop. Over and over, she sang, "Amazing grace, how sweet the sound that saved a wretch like me; I once was lost but now I'm found; was blind but now I see".

It was all very unusual entering into the bookshop. Naomi had always considered Christians to be daggy and very uncool. As soon as she got to the shelf she was looking for, little Billy began screaming in the pram and it began to feel awkward looking for a bible while rocking the pram. The screams got louder, and she saw out of the corner of her eye a man walking towards her. He was wearing cut off denim shorts, work boots and a scruffy dusty ripped t-shirt.

"Hi there, you go to our church, don't you? I'll take the pram while you look if you like. Do you know what you are looking for?" he asked.

Billy stopped screaming and Naomi found the bible she wanted. Naomi headed toward the counter to pay for it and tried to take the pram back off the man. He again offered to help until she had paid and was organised. Thanking him and remembering him as the guy who sat at the back of the church each week, she walked to her car. The man followed and assisted her as she strapped Billy in, put her bags in and got organised.

After clipping Billy into his seat, she threw her handbag on the front seat and proceeded to drive out of the carpark. That familiar voice echoed again to Naomi and this time it said, "Can you see the difference? He is one of mine."

"Oh," thought Naomi. "What does that mean? Does that mean that Tom wasn't?"

She didn't know and it was too much for her to continue to think about right now. Nevertheless, it was her God again whispering to her at one of the most important parts of her life. This hope, this chance meeting in a Christian bookshop, opposed to a café in Greece. Two different men and little did she know she would be comparing these encounters in the years to follow.

Naomi spent every day and every night reading her bible while breastfeeding her baby. Naomi felt she too was drinking milk, the milk of God. Just like her milk was keeping her new baby alive so were the promises of God's milk keeping her alive, feeding her with hope and joy and encouraging her in every living way.

"I can't wait for Tom to come," she thought one day after praying for him. She mentioned this to Lisa, a girl she chatted with at church. Lisa was a straight shooter and not one to hold back when it came to sharing her faith with other new believers.

"What do you pray for him for? Why do you waste your breath? I don't know why you bother. I think you are wasting your time, to be honest, praying for him," Lisa saic.

"He is the father of my son and I believe God loves family and I believe he will come one day," Naomi replied.

"Listen, Naomi," said Lisa, repeatedly trying to speak some sense to her but with no empathy or warmth. "What you need to be praying is for God to open or close doors in that relationship! You can't sit around praying for what you want forever. You need to know where you stand so you can move on with your life."

"Okay," sighed Naomi. "Will you pray with me?"

Together Naomi and Lisa prayed that God would either open or close the door with Tom so she could have some closure or something to look forward to. It was a scary thing to pray, and Naomi was convinced without a doubt that God could see, hear, and understand all things pertaining to life on earth and she knew he loved her right where she was at.

With that faith, she closed her eyes and began to ask God to intervene in this area of her life and give her the answers she needed.

Chapter 11 – Valentine's Day

It was on Valentine's Day, just ten days after the scary prayer, that Naomi received a letter in the mail from Tom. Looking at the envelope and looking up to the sky, she knew God had heard her prayer.

"How nice," she said, "and it even arrived on Valentine's Day."

Opening the letter and flopping down on the couch, Naomi registered it was not the news she had been hoping for; in fact, it was the complete opposite.

A horrible sinking feeling began to take over her as she read the letter. She read the letter over again for a second time. Tom was now married to his former girlfriend, and they had a child. How could that be?

"Find a husband in your newfound religion and get on with the rest of your life," the letter said. It was one big, long page of instruction and rejection. It was signed, "Leave me and my family alone."

No love, no romance, no charm, no wit, no humour this time.

Anger began to rise and all hope in the promise of God attempted to leave her heart and mind.

"What is this all about?" she screamed.

Her friend, Angela, had just arrived and just in time too. Angela was a young university student who attended the same church and lived in the area.

"Well," Angela said. "God must have better things in store for you."

"What?" asked Naomi. "As if there could be anything better than marrying the father of your child and being a family."

"Well, what hope have you got, Naomi? Jesus is your only hope," continued Angela. "You have nothing else, do you? You have a choice to hang on to hope or let it go, your choice. The hope that is God, the hope that is Christ Jesus Himself."

"I am stuffed," Naomi said to herself.

Angela went on to say, "Rest in the knowledge of God and you will see in time that God was guiding your steps. At least you know God hears your prayers, Naomi. That's got to be a good thing, hasn't it? You will see that God works all things together for good to those who love Him and to those who are called according to His purpose."

"Yeah, whatever. See you later," said Naomi, waving her off.

Angela drove off and thought to herself, "I hope she hangs on."

Naomi thought to herself, "I have ruined my life and an innocent life too. This poor little baby. Where do I go from here?"

Wiping her tears and feeding her baby, she tried to rewind her life and make a list of all the things she had done wrong and all the people she had hurt over her life. The list was longer than she expected, and she wept at the hurt she had caused other people.

"Perhaps I have reaped what I have sowed," she pondered.

Chapter 12 – New friends

Church picnics were kind of goofy to Naomi; however, she couldn't deny the love the people radiated. They loved one another and they loved her. There were certainly some odd characters among the group. They reminded her of a bag of mixed lollies—all sweet but all different. The church group were just like that—a bag of all sorts. The people were all so different, but it was their individual stories that she loved. Other people's stories brought her hope and she felt she was safe with other people who had had a similar supernatural experience with Jesus Christ. Unlike some of her old friends, these people had experienced the same depth of sorrow and some loss but also had experienced the same level of joy and elation in their newfound hope and love of God.

This like-minded connection cemented her new friendships, and she began to experience a steady flow of constant invitations to coffee, lunch, dinner, picnics, and the like. Naomi was out and about and living a very busy social life again but this time it was different. Naomi had bought a portable cot and set it up for Billy wherever she went. Little Billy had learnt to sleep here, there, and anywhere including on the side of the river while Naomi went swimming and fishing.

This lifestyle brought no routine, no structure and this was just the way Naomi liked it. Her lifestyle was wild but in a different kind of way; wild in faith and somewhat eccentric.

Naomi formed many strong friendships during Billy's early days. These God-given friendships did help heal her broken heart and kept her busy. With the change of direction in her life, her sad moments began to get less and less, and her outlook on life brightened.

An invitation to Kim and Dave's sparked up something very new.

"Just bring something to drink," smiled Kim, "and we'll see you about three."

While she was feeding Billy one teaspoon at a time and wiping his mouth, Kim and Dave opened their front door to the man she had seen at the bookshop.

"Oh, hello," he said. "I'm Bruce; I met you at the bookshop. What's your name again?"

Kim and Dave went to introduce Bruce and it seemed that they had met but had not exchanged names. Naomi stayed in the kitchen with the babies while everyone else was outside enjoying the summer and the barbecue.

"Are you coming outside?" invited Kim.

"Oh, no, thanks. I'll just stay inside with the babies," Naomi said.

Kim looked confused and said, "But they are all asleep."

Naomi was not sure how to behave in mixed company. In her old life, she was so used to showing off and knew how to draw attention to herself that she struggled to join in. She knew she could be herself with woman but with men she didn't feel she could trust them and was not sure she ever wanted to again. In fact, now she wasn't sure she even wanted to be at the barbecue. She got herself a hotdog and sat down amongst a group of people and the conversations began to flow. Naomi sensed some people judging her and others checking her out. She didn't like it. It became apparent she was with mixed company in more ways than one. Everyone else was married except her and Bruce; at least, she didn't think he was married. Naomi wasn't sure she enjoyed the atmosphere. She really didn't like being with other married couples, especially ones who had babies the same age as hers.

Looking around and scouting out the scene, she thought she would go home. Bruce asked her a couple of questions but nothing too deep. It was Kim and Sue who spoke a timely word of encouragement and so she changed her mind and stayed longer and was eventually the last person to go home after Bruce. Driving home, Naomi realised this new life was different to her old life. Some parts she liked and other parts of it she was very unsure of. These thoughts went around and around in her mind but the good parts about her new life brought her back again to hope. After all, what did she have outside of her new faith and this new circle of friends? She had nothing else.

Chapter 13 – Bruce

Seeing the girls from playgroup was great.

"It is important," she thought, "that I don't wipe these old friends off."

Her new life was busy; it had kept her away from her old friends and Naomi decided, after spending a day with Justine, that it was time to do something for others. So much had been done for her and she thought it was time to clean her dad's house and have a dinner party, Naomi hadn't ever held a dinner party, but she knew that with the help of her new friend, Julie, she could pull it off.

After inviting a few friends around including Rebecca who had had a baby at 16 and was also on her own as her boyfriend was off with his mates, Bruce came to mind so she thought she would invite him too. He asked if he could bring his friend Daniel and his girlfriend too.

"No problem," thought Naomi. "The more the merrier."

Naomi couldn't believe it when Daniel arrived. He was the old boyfriend of Justine, a friend of hers, and the father of Charlie. Justine was also a single mum on her own and Daniel was off with his new girlfriend and now at Naomi's place for dinner. It was clear that Bruce and Naomi had similar friends, although they had not known each other.

"This is unbelievable," Naomi said to Julie in the kitchen. "How can I explain this to Justine?"

Justine had only rung an hour before to say she could not come to dinner because Charlie was unwell.

"Was that a God thing?" thought Naomi. The only conclusion was perhaps this was. These God things were happening often, and it couldn't all be possibly a coincidence. Bruce had been praying for his friend, Daniel, while Naomi was heartbroken for her friend, Justine, from playgroup. Naomi had been praying for Justine too.

Everyone had a great time, and it was after washing up the dishes that Naomi asked Bruce how he knew Daniel. It had turned out that he had worked with him on a few building sites and caught up with him among mutual old friends now and then.

Pondering this the following day, Naomi thought that perhaps God was wanting her to pray for them both in the hope that maybe Justine and Daniel could reconcile, reunite, get married and live happily ever after. Little did Naomi know that day that that's exactly what would happen.

The following Sunday after church, Bruce invited Naomi, Julie, and Geoff over for dinner. He was making chilli con carne. Bruce shared a bachelor-pad with Dale, Scott, and Paul.

"Wow," thought Naomi. She was thinking how cool a man who can cook was. She was so glad Julie and Geoff were invited as she would never have gone on her own.

Naomi packed an extra bottle for Billy and some food and off she went, following Julie and Geoff's car to Bruce's place. There were at least 12 people in such a small house but Naomi thought it was great warm hospitality.

Naomi didn't talk much, just ate and cuddled Billy until the coffee and chocolates came out. Once again, everyone shared their stories,

stories of great sorrow and despair followed by the wonder and hope of the invitation to follow Jesus.

"So, we are all guests really at the invisible table of the Lord. These must be like my brothers and sisters," thought Naomi. "We are like a family but stronger and connected deeply, deeper than the things of this earth."

It was way too much to think about.

The understanding about caring for one another was deeply profound that night. Naomi watched as each person strengthened the others as they opened their heart and authentically shared their faith journey.

Julie, Geoff, and Naomi all left at the same time and, as Julie and Geoff were parked behind Naomi, they drove off first.

Bruce came to Naomi's window and said, "Thanks for coming," and he hoped she had a good time. Bruce mentioned there were many things about Naomi he admired and asked if he could call her for a chat in the week. Naomi was glad the sun had gone down and it was dark as her face was fiery red and she squirmed in her car seat at the compliment from Bruce.

"Bye, Billy," he waved as Billy sat in the car sear and they smiled as Naomi drove off home to Mullaloo.

"Why do I feel like I am 12 again?" questioned Naomi to God on the way home. "I feel so awkward."

What on earth could she talk about with Bruce when he phoned? She didn't do anything exciting throughout the day and besides why did he want to talk to her?

The following day Bruce called Naomi after work and they chatted for hours. There was more that could be said without people listening to every word like in church or in groups with the others. Naomi sympathised with Bruce about his drug use as a teenager prior to his encounter with Christ and his insane mother and the highs and lows of life in general. After hearing more about Bruce's life, Naomi felt better about herself.

"You know, Naomi, don't feel condemned about having a baby out of wedlock. Everyone at church has had sex outside of marriage and it could have happened to anyone. You just happened to fall pregnant. Aren't you glad you did? You wouldn't have gorgeous Billy and you may never had met God if your life had been different," Bruce said.

Naomi knew he was right, and she was comforted by his words. He had stirred up hope again and demonstrated love just as she had seen all the other Christians do.

"Would you like to go out for dinner on Friday night? Do you like Mexican? I know a great place we can go and it's not far from you. I will come and pick you and Billy up if you want to go?" he asked.

At six thirty on the dot, Bruce arrived to pick up Naomi and Billy. Just like he said he would, Bruce arrived with 12 red roses and Naomi was embarrassed.

"I don't have any vases," she said awkwardly. Thanking Bruce and remembering the green plastic bucket in the laundry, she used for Billy's nappies she filled it with water and put the roses in.

Bruce was different: A new kind of friend, clearly from a different class of people but still gracious and he made Naomi feel comfortable. Bruce sensed Naomi was still a bit fragile and so he was careful with her and intentional when it came to conversation. Bruce loved Naomi's simple heart. He thought she was uncomplicated and naturally happy.

At the restaurant, Bruce asked the waiter for a highchair for Billy and the three of them sat down and enjoyed the Mexican experience. With Billy throwing food from the highchair to the table and across to nearby tables, Bruce was entertained.

Sensing Naomi was embarrassed, Bruce said, "You know when I ask you out, I never want you to get a babysitter. When I invite you I want you to know that always includes Billy."

The patrons in the restaurant were amused at this fun-loving baby. As the eyes turned towards their table, Naomi realised that everyone in the restaurant would be thinking they were a family. They looked like a happy family having fun. Naomi enjoyed the moment and treasured the care.

Winter arrived and Naomi stayed inside her dad's house more, lighting the fire and again reading anything and everything pertaining to Godliness. More content with life and herself, she began eating chocolates and drinking Milos with marshmallows, baking cakes, pies and experimenting in the kitchen.

After parking her car in the carport one wild windy afternoon, she had just got inside the house when there was an enormous bang and crash outside her house. Opening the curtains, she stared with goosebumps rushing up and down her body. The large gumtree had fallen over into the driveway right where Naomi normally parked her car. Just 10 minutes before she had been standing there and had chosen to park in the carport so she could get Billy out of car without getting wet as it was pouring down.

Thoughts flashed through her mind. It was another chance—what if Billy had been in the car or worse, both of them? The storm was settling in and so she thanked God and locked herself in the house and lit the wood fire. There was nothing she could do now, but at least the car was okay in the carport and she and Billy were alive.

Bruce phoned later that evening and she shared what happened. Bruce said he would come by after work and pick up a chainsaw and move the tree. Naomi's dad was away and there was no one else offering to help. Bruce arrived and soon the gumtree was chopped up and cleared out of the way.

"What are you having for dinner tonight?" asked Bruce.

"Oh, just a sandwich," Naomi replied.

His eyes of mercy glanced over to her kitchen, and he suggested he go to the shops and buy the ingredients and come back and cook her a meal.

"Thank you," said Naomi and added, protecting herself, "but my mum is planning on coming over tonight. I can see if she would like to join us."

Naomi's mum was intimidated by Bruce. He was self-confident and not anything like the sleazebags at the pub.

Bruce cooked steak Diane and garlic sauce, stuffed tomatoes, and vegetables. It was so delicious, and Naomi knew it was an expensive dinner and thought about what it would have cost. The rump steak was so tender.

"I could get use to this," she smiled to herself.

Bruce was constantly inviting Naomi to picnics and dinners and, as long as Naomi was surrounded with a group of people, she accepted. She wasn't ready for one-to-one dates even though she trusted Bruce.

Seven weeks after their home-cooked dinner together, without Naomi knowing she had made it into Bruce's heart and all he could think of night and day was of her and the welfare of her little baby, Billy. Bruce couldn't believe someone would let go of someone so beautiful, so kind and so happy. Bruce understood though the selfish heart of any human and, given the right or wrong circumstances, anything dark was possible including what had happened to Naomi.

Chapter 14 – The proposal

One Sunday morning sitting close to the front of the church, the music began. Naomi had a favourite worship song and, as she sang the song with all of her heart, tears began to fall down her face as she considered again the hope that Christ had brought to her. She was feeling so grateful when that same voice spoke to her as she clasped her hands in front of her mouth. It said, "Bruce will ask you to marry him tonight."

"I think I am going mad," she thought as drove home after church. It was the same still voice that had spoken to her in her room that night. Naomi did not say anything to anyone at the thought that she could possibly be going mad and hearing voices.

That evening Bruce asked her if she would like to go for a drive to Scarborough and get an ice-cream. He knew of this new gourmet ice-cream shop and wanted to treat her to one and share the experience. After changing Billy into his pyjamas, they set off for one of the super-duper ice creams.

"I'm having the Cookie Cream Commotion," said Bruce.

"I'll have the Old English Toffee," said Naomi, "please."

Returning to the car with their ice-creams, they sat and stared out to sea. Billy was fast asleep in the car seat and the silence was unusual.

"Naomi, there are so many things about you that I really like,. Would you like to be my wife?" Bruce smiled and then continued to look forward out to the waves crashing in front of him.

Naomi froze, looked forward and said nothing.

After a long awkward pause, Bruce interrupted with, "You don't have to tell me now if you don't want to. You can let me know later if you want to think about it."

Fumbling through her handbag for nothing at all, Naomi hesitated and then said, "Yes, all right. I'm not doing anything else now."

Bruce laughed and proceeded to drive Naomi home.

"Well, I will see you later in the week," said Bruce, "and we can go and pick out an engagement ring if you like."

"Okay, thanks. See you later," said Naomi and shut the front door.

She fell on the couch and thought, "How bloody weird."

She had never kissed Bruce or held his hand and here he was asking her to marry him. How backward, how upside down, how different, but something in her knew how very right it was and she skipped off to bed.

Naomi picked out an engagement ring and Bruce said he would pick it up for her on payday and drop it off.

The following Thursday, Bruce did just that—picked up the engagement ring, took it over to Naomi's and handed her the ring like it was a postage stamp. Naomi opened the box, placed the ring on her finger and thanked Bruce with a kiss on the cheek.

"So, would you like a coffee?" Naomi asked him.

"Just a quick one, I can't stay. I have to go to my grandmother's," he replied.

The following week, they went out for coffee to discuss the wedding arrangements. The date was chosen for two reasons. One was that Julie was having a baby and Naomi thought it was only right that she was a bridesmaid and the other was that Naomi's dad would be back from his job around October so they set October 23rd as the date. It was only 11 weeks away.

It was obvious Bruce wanted to do the right thing according to his newfound faith and save intimacy for the wedding night; however, it was obvious to Naomi that he didn't want to leave it any longer than necessary.

Naomi laughed one morning when putting the cats outside. She found a note at the front door. Bruce had dropped off a list of his relatives and some money for invitations on his way to work.

As Naomi wrote out the invitations, she realised she had never met any of the people on his lists. Bruce's dad roared with mocking laughter when he told him he was marrying Naomi. His dad was a car salesman and had mentioned that most buyers take second-hand cars for a good run before purchasing. He mentioned that marrying Naomi should be no different.

Bruce was insulted but understood his father was dead in his sins and with no understanding of spiritual things or God, for that matter, so his response was to be expected.

Bruce continued to go around to his family and share his good news. With some of the feedback he received, it was decided not to have an engagement party. It was clear not many family members were pleased or understood the decision.

Naomi's mother was suspicious while Naomi's friends thought she was desperate and running into the arms of the first man to show her kindness. Nevertheless, they were set apart from the things that normally made sense to them now that they were understanding thing from God's perspective and were both committed to God and his new path for them.

The wedding went ahead: The dress was pretty, the limo great, the photos came out nice, the church was okay, and the reception was a complete flop.

Leaving the reception after 45 minutes, fear entered Naomi's mind. She was feeling sick and very nervous. With no alcohol or dancing at the reception, it did not feel like much of a celebration and now she was panicking. Naomi's mum had lent her the use of her MG sports car for the honeymoon and thoughts of driving to the country in her mum's cool sports car had excited Naomi. Next morning at valet parking, more bad news arrived—the clutch on the MG was stuck and a porter delivered the news that they could not get the car out of valet parking and were advised to get a mechanic on to it straight away.

Returning from the honeymoon early after missing Billy, they laughed about their adventure in the old ute and the wedding but were both happy to be moving into a unit together with Billy.

Chapter 15 – The Brown family

Thirty years passed and Bruce and Naomi went on to have two children, siblings for Billy. Josh and Billy were best brothers and best friends, and they adored their little sister, Rosie. There were many happy years as a family learning about the things of God and working hard to go on holidays and enjoy all the things life had to offer. The family never went without, and their home overflowed with every good thing as was promised by God.

However, for the first 14 years of Billy's life, on each birthday Naomi would shed a tear at some point during the day. It was sometimes first thing in the morning before the family awoke, or after cleaning up from one of Billy's birthday parties. Shedding tears was something Naomi did on her own, never with Bruce or the other children.

It was on Billy's 14th birthday, after church, that a stranger noticed her crying and came up to her to offer support. After briefly sharing her situation, the stranger spoke powerful words of comfort to Naomi. The last thing the stranger said after a time was, "This will be the last birthday you will ever feel like this."

"Thanks "said Naomi and wandered off, thinking it meant she would be stronger next birthday and not make a public fool of herself.

It wasn't too long after Billy's 14th birthday that her dad called to say he was having a clean-out and had come across some footage of her and Tom in Greece.

"Thanks for letting me know, Dad, but throw it away. I am not interested in it," Naomi said.

Strangely, that particular week, Billy had been asking questions about her moral values as a young woman and interrogating her regarding his conception. During the retelling of her story to Billy, she recalled the conversation she had with her father about the video footage.

Without hesitating, Naomi called her dad back and requested he save the footage and that she would pick it up some time during that week.

The time came and Naomi and Billy watched the footage alone. Billy saw what he needed and said, "Thanks, Mum. That's enough. Turn it off, please."

Although he saw the footage, it was not enough for Billy. More questions stirred his heart and upset his week. Processing the loss and the grief was not easy for either of them during this time.

It was around this time that the internet became a global tool for communication, with interesting new ways of rediscovering lost friends and family. Naomi suggested to Billy that Tom might be able to be located. *Friends Reunited Australia, New Zealand and UK* popped up and, without hesitation, Naomi typed in his name. In an instant, up came Tom including a photograph of his face. She mentioned to Billy what she had discovered and together they decided to send a short message regarding the video footage of Greece they had seen.

Excited but very nervous, Billy took over the keyboard and began to communicate with Tom.

Tom presented as being very pleased to hear from Tom and the communication started.

As pleasing as this was to Billy, it was not long before it began to be a thorn in his flesh. Tom was now married again, had two other children and was living in Ireland.

After the initial connection, rejection presented again after Billy suggested he was now an adult and would like to visit Tom face-to-face and meet his family.

Time went on and more new ways to connect online via Facebook presented. Billy, in his own time, began to explore and discovered his other half-brothers and sisters who Tom had had with Lesley, his first wife, before abandoning them also and fleeing without any communication.

He made a connection with his half-siblings and a trip to London to visit this part of his family was planned.

The trip was comforting, and Billy returned with a new sense of belonging, feeling that he belonged to his family on all sides.

Epilogue

A life lived well is a great way to honour those who gave us life, not to mention the Author and Finisher of our life on earth.

Billy went on and lived a fulfilled life of adventure, took every opportunity to succeed seriously and made a lasting impression on every person he met.

Gratitude and humility in all things became the outlook for Naomi and Bruce. They too travelled, studied and took every opportunity to improve and succeed in chosen careers.

Continuing to share their faith experience and journey with all who were interested, Naomi and Bruce lived a content life together, remembering to pray when trials presented and give thanks when the going was good.

Nurture or nature, chance, or choice, the mysteries of God and life on earth continued to present. No day was the same, but each day was a new day filled with hope. Bruce and Naomi were never ones to look back, always choosing to hold hands, look up and continue to believe for good things for themselves and their family. Holding the promises of God in their hearts, they boldly continued believing there were many good things yet for them to discover.

Not caring what they may appear to the world but like children playing on the seashore, diverting in finding smoother pebbles and prettier shells while the great ocean of truth lay all undiscovered before them; well, at least some of the truth.

Afterword

It is my privilege to share my faith and I hope those who read my story also find comfort. Life happens to us all and we cannot escape this life without some trial or disappointment. The disappointment can be viewed as a crossroad, the crossroad of choice, one of opportunity. I recommend calling out to the God who created the heavens, the earth and everything in it. Repent of your sins and the bad choices we all have and ask for forgiveness. Our sin has been paid for by the blood of Jesus Christ. All we have to do is repent and wait on the Lord. His promises will overtake you if you choose to put him and His kingdom first. There is no other way. Jesus says, "I am the way, the truth, and the life. All who call upon me will have life and life more abundant."

Rest in the promises of God and take comfort in your own history (His story) for you.

Vanessa Adelaide

About the Author

Vanessa is a therapeutic social worker and enjoys working with vulnerable people and communities. Vanessa not only uses her professional study background but personal experience as a tool to support and provide hope to all who come to her. *A Crossroad Destiny* is another tool written with the intention of supporting all who have ears to hear.

Vanessa is also the author of several children's books including:

My Lonely Dolly
The Blue Crayon
The Old Teddy
The Red truck
Connor the Kangaroo from Kalgoorlie
Nana Loves Dress Ups
A Cat Called Harvey.

Using the stories as an analogy into the real world, Vanessa believes her stories can be used as a tool to have difficult conversations with children.

www.ingramcontent.com/pod-product-compliance
Lightning Source LLC
Chambersburg PA
CBHW061335040426
42444CB00011B/2940